A Pilgrim's Gu...
THE HOLY LAND
ISRAEL AND JORDAN

By Raymond Goodburn

Pilgrim Book Services Limited

© Pilgrim Book Services Limited and Raymond Goodburn 2010
ISBN 978-0-9532511-6-2

Published by Pilgrim Book Services Ltd., P.O. Box 27, Woodbridge, Suffolk, England IP13 9AU

 www.pilgrimbooks.com

Designed by Bob Vickers
Cover design by Fielding Design
Maps by Rodney Paull

Printed in Great Britain by Colourstream Litho Ltd.

Mixed Sources
Product group from well-managed
forests and other controlled sources
www.fsc.org Cert no. SGS-COC-004224
© 1996 Forest Stewardship Council
FSC

This third edition is substantially revised from the second edition published in 1998, during which and since the authors and publishers received invaluable assistance from the Israel Government Tourist Office; similarly from the Jordan Tourism Board and the London office of Royal Jordanian Airlines.
Part 8 The Flora and Fauna of the Holy Land, an article contributed by the late Margaret Smith, is reproduced for this edition with the agreement of the Revd Raymond Smith.
All photos from page 4 onwards are the author's own.

Cover picture: View through the window of the Church of Dominus Flevit

CONTENTS

Part 1 SETTING THE SCENE   **5**
The Meaning of Pilgrimage
Where Three Faiths Meet
The People of the Holy Land
The Geography of Israel
A Historical Perspective

Part 2 IN AND AROUND JERUSALEM   **14**
Topography
The Walls
Outside the Walls
The Mount of Olives
The Old City – Christian Sites and the Via Dolorosa
The Temple Area – Moslem and Jewish Shrines
The Events of Holy Week
Exploring East Jerusalem
West Jerusalem

Part 3 JOURNEYS FROM JERUSALEM   **35**
Bethlehem – Hebron – Herodion
Emmaus and Bethany
South to Beersheba and Eilat
The Dead Sea – Masada – Qumran
North to Galilee via the West Bank and Samaria
North to Galilee via Jericho and the Jordan Valley

Part 4 THE GALILEE   **48**
Lower Galilee
Around the Lake
Upper Galilee

Part 5 THE COASTAL PLAIN 59

Part 6 FOR FURTHER INFORMATION – ISRAEL 62

Part 7 JORDAN 70
The Background
Of People, Politics and Economics
A Potted Biblical History
Beginning in Amman
The Cities of the Decapolis
Jerash
The Desert Castles
The King's Highway
Petra
Aqaba and Wadi Rum
Practical information for Jordan

Part 8 THE FLORA AND FAUNA OF THE HOLY LAND 94

Inside the Church of the Holy Sepulchre

Part 1
SETTING THE SCENE

THE MEANING OF PILGRIMAGE

This book is a re-write and update of several previous editions written by my friend and colleague David Houseley, who has now handed on to me the mantle of authorship, and to whom I am greatly indebted for much that is in this new version. Between us we have led or taken part in more than sixty Pilgrimage Tours to the Holy Land, with a wide variety of Clergy and people from every conceivable denomination, so there is a wealth of experience behind what is written.

One of the main things I have discovered is that a Pilgrimage Tour means different things to different people. There are elements within the experience which you may place in a differing order of importance, either from the priorities of your travelling companions or even your Tour Leader. So this following list of priorities may not necessarily be the same as yours, but here they are!

... A Pilgrimage Tour is first and foremost an enjoyable holiday, but one which has something special to offer the traveller – it is a holiday with a particular purpose and therefore with added meaning.

... One of the major reasons for enjoyment is the fellowship of like-minded people with whom you are travelling.

... It offers the opportunity of a spiritual re-awakening and a re-affirmation of faith, or as a Palestinian Christian guide from Bethlehem once put it to one of my groups, 'We are here to deepen our faith and polish our spirits'.

The order of these elements may surprise you, especially those who regard such a tour mainly as a spiritual retreat. But for most it will be primarily a holiday, and a holiday is for relaxation and refreshment, of the body as well as the mind and the spirit. So go with a determination to enjoy it.

The fellowship with your travelling companions will come both in the informal chats over meals and relaxing over a drink in the evenings, as well as through the acts of corporate worship and devotion which most groups will share together at the various sites. It is this sharing of experiences and insights which makes a visit to the Holy Land such a special journey.

As for the spiritual re-awakening, it is inconceivable that you will visit this land without the background to the Bible, and the ministry of Jesus in particular, coming alive in a unique way and without your faith being refreshed. When, for example, you stand on the Mount of Olives and look towards Jerusalem, it is impossible not to picture that final entry of Jesus into the city on what we now call Palm Sunday; or when you stand on the summit of Mount Nebo in Jordan and look across into Israel as Moses did, when he saw the Promised Land which he would never enter. Places that you have previously only read about inform your understanding, not only while you are in the Holy Land, but subsequently when you return home and read about those places which you yourself have visited and experienced. These are the kinds of moments, and there will be many, which will remain in your memory for ever and make the hackneyed phrase, 'Journey of a Lifetime', ring true for you.

There is something to be said for not over-preparing or reading too much in advance, though clearly you will want to do something of both, but rather to let the various sites speak for themselves and make their own impression on you, and then do the detailed reading later. Furthermore, remember that a visit to the Holy Land is not just about particular piles of stones in particular places. If you go with that expectation you will often be disappointed. Rather, let your focus be on the holy event behind the holy place, in other words, what a particular holy place represents and the faith it inspires. Reading the Bible, and notably the Gospels, will never be quite the same again – it will become a picture book of memories as you read about places and events which have made their own special impact on you.

The aim of this book, as with others in the Pilgrim series, is to be compact, concise, colourful and informative. It does not set out to be excessively academic or highly detailed in its descriptions, nor does it have any particular theological slant. Its intention is to say just enough for you to identify where you are and hopefully be a stimulus for further reading later. As someone who is firmly ecumenical in outlook, I hope this book will be of value to pilgrims of various denominations, as well as encouraging a deeper understanding of the traditions of other faiths whose followers also worship the one God in this Holy Land. I hope, too, that you will find it a handy and helpful aid while you are there, and a souvenir recalling many memories for long after you return home.

Raymond Goodburn

WHERE THREE FAITHS MEET

This book is intended primarily for the Christian Pilgrim to the Holy Land and, therefore, assumes that the reader is familiar with the teaching of the Bible and especially the major events of the life and ministry of Jesus. Your acceptance is also assumed of Jesus as the Son of God, the Messiah, who in his birth, life, death and resurrection laid down the basis for the redemption of humankind. But the Christian visitor must also realise that the Holy Land in general, and Jerusalem in particular, has no less significance for those of other faiths, notably Islam and Judaism, both of which share some common ground and, therefore, some of the sites you will visit, with Christianity. Indeed, Jerusalem is a meeting point for these three monotheistic faiths.

ISLAM

Islam takes as its basis the simple creed that 'There is no God but Allah, and Mohammed is his messenger'. Mohammed lived from 570–632 AD. Jerusalem is very sacred to Moslems, coming after Mecca and Medina as the third Holy Place, because Mohammed visited it in his 'Night Vision' and it contains the Dome of the Rock and the nearby El Aksa Mosque. Islamic Articles of Faith are: a belief in God, the Almighty and Merciful; the existence of angels; the Book of the Quran (in which there is a description of the birth of Jesus); the prophets, including Adam, Noah, Abraham, Moses, Jesus and Mohammed; the Resurrection to Judgement; and Heaven and Hell.

The practical duties, known as the Pillars of Islam, are five in number:

1. Declaration of Faith in the One-ness of God and in the Divine Messengership of Mohammed.
2. Formal prayer.
3. Fasting during the month of Ramadan.
4. Almsgiving.
5. Pilgrimage to the Holy City of Mecca.

JUDAISM

Jews believe that the Messiah has not yet come. Judaism began as a Covenant between God and Abraham, and later with the whole people, as represented by Moses on Mount Sinai. The Covenant is often broken by humans but is always renewed by God with his chosen people – Israel. Jewish belief centres on the one and only God, omnipotent and omnipresent. Israel is a holy nation, chosen to proclaim God's holiness to all people and to promote obedience to him. The Messiah will come to establish God's kingdom on earth and this will be consummated in the world to come. The main duties, both moral and ceremonial, are represented in the Ten Commandments. At the heart of Judaism is obedience to the Torah, which is divided into the written and the oral law. The written Torah (or Pentateuch) is

Arabs, Jews and Christians share the Holy Land

found in the first five books of the Bible, and the oral law is the Talmud. The Talmud is a combination of Mishna (a record of discussions between Rabbis in the first two centuries AD) and Gemara (an explanation of the Mishna by Rabbis who lived some generations later). The New Testament is not regarded as divine revelation by Jews, but all the books of what Christians call the Old Testament are what Judaism accepts as the Bible. Jesus is honoured as a prophet, but not as Messiah or Son of God.

It is for the Christian visitor to seek the common ground between these faiths, rather than to dwell on the divisions. It is all too easy, even within Holy Places, to find divisions within Christianity itself, but it is far more rewarding to seek the bonds which draw people together. It is in such a spirit that the pilgrim will learn most and so find spiritual refreshment and a re-affirmation of faith.

THE PEOPLE OF THE HOLY LAND

To the casual visitor there are Arabs and there are Jews. But life is far more complex than that. In fact, the people comprising the land could hardly be more varied. There are, for instance:

The Bedouin   The proud, independent, nomadic tribes who inhabit the deserts in the summer and the protective valleys in the winter. The majority are now settled, but many can still be seen living in their black goat-skin tents, or driving herds of sheep and goats to find a sparse pasture.

The Fellahim   The settled Arabs, whose dress is a flowing gown, called 'aba', a long shirt – 'thawb', and the head shawl and cord – 'kufiyah' and 'igal'. In public the women are less in evidence than the men and usually cover their faces. The national drink, coffee, is always offered as a symbol of welcome.

The Druze   A fanatical and war-like race, their men are handsome and the women strikingly beautiful. They accept a faith made up of parts of Islam, Judaism and Christianity, but with a closely guarded set of 'mysteries'. Their sacred shrine is the Tomb of Jethro.

The Sephardim   These are descended from Jews who were expelled from Spain in 1492 at the time of the Inquisition and who settled in various places around the Mediterranean. One of their centres is at Safed in Galilee, to which they have brought a distinctive intellectual and artistic flavour. After the Second World War thousands also came to Israel from North Africa and the Balkans.

Ashkenazim   German Jews who, in the 15th and 16th centuries, migrated to Poland and Russia but kept the Yiddish language. They began to settle in the

Holy Land in the 19th century and the influx from Eastern Europe post-1945 was immense. They formed the first farm communities and later the kibbutzim, and from their ranks came the most influential Zionists who helped create the modern State of Israel.

Anglo Saxon Jews   Though comparatively small in number they have been influential in business and professional life, and in the kibbutzim.

Central Europeans   A more recent and sophisticated immigrant, they left Europe during the rise of Nazism to found the city of Tel Aviv and populate the coastal area.

Samaritans Occupiers of the land after the fall of Israel, they accepted only the Pentateuch and chose Mt. Gerizim as their holy place in preference to Jerusalem. The few remaining Samaritans still celebrate their Passover on this mountain top near Nablus.

The Asians These have poured into Israel since Independence, fleeing from persecution in Iraq or Persia, as it was, many coming in specially organised airlifts. Some 50,000 Yemenites were flown from Aden in 1949 and brought with them special skills in wood, metal work, pottery and embroidery. The Yemenites have a striking and colourful costume and have contributed greatly to the emergence of Israeli folk music.

The Sabra   Though a nickname this is a title proudly borne, for it was originally applied to those first generation Jews who were born in the State of Israel, though it is now used to describe anyone who is a native Israeli-Jew.

In more recent times there have been spectacular evacuations of black African Jews from Uganda and Ethiopia. These latest, the Falashas, claim to be one of the lost tribes of Israel as descendants of Solomon and the Queen of Sheba. The easing of east-west relations also brought a large influx of Jews from Russia and other east European countries. It is this diversity of background which makes Israel such a fascinating mix of peoples.

However, it should not be thought that, given such variety, the Jewish religion provides a unifying element. Far from it! While there is a powerful minority who believe that the State of Israel should be founded on the laws laid down in the Torah, the majority, nevertheless, regard this as totally unacceptable. For them, Israel is primarily a secular and not a religious state.

THE GEOGRAPHY OF ISRAEL

PHYSICAL FEATURES
Israel consists of a central spine of hills, with the coastal plain bordering the Mediterranean to the west and the Jordan Valley, which forms part of the great

Rift Valley, to the east. Beyond the Valley, in the Kingdom of Jordan, are the Biblical lands of Edom, Moab and Gilead, a country of mountains and deep ravines leading to a desert plateau on the borders with Syria, Iraq and Saudi Arabia. Israel itself has four distinctive regions:

The Coastal Plain   Varying in width from five miles in the north to 25 miles in the south, this is the fertile land of agriculture, orchards and vineyards. Between the Ladder of Tyre and Mt. Carmel is the plain of Acre; between Carmel and Tel Aviv the plain of Sharon; and further south to Gaza is the plain of Philistia. But it was not always fertile and much of it was reclaimed from swamp by the early settlers.

The Central Range   The high plateau of Upper Galilee, under the shadow of Mt. Hermon (9200 ft), falls abruptly to the hill country of Lower Galilee and the Sea of Galilee, which is nearly 700 ft below sea level. Between Galilee and the softer Samaritan hills is a triangular plain, Emek Jezreel, which is known as Israel's breadbasket, the only flat area where cereal crops can be profitably grown. Further south the Samaritan hills merge into those of Judea, which become both higher and wilder.

The Jordan Valley   Three separate sources of the river join just south of Mt. Hermon, before it descends some 687 ft in less than nine miles to flow into the Sea of Galilee. It leaves the Sea at its southernmost point and forms part of the boundary between Israel and Jordan before falling another 600 ft to the Dead Sea, meandering in a valley within a valley for some 200 miles, though the distance as the crow flies is but 65 miles.

The Negev ('Dry Land')   This vast area south of the hills of Judea is steppe land, much of its northern part now being irrigated. It merges beyond Beersheba into desert and arid mountains, finally bordering the Red Sea at the fashionable resort of Eilat.

The question of the land and who owns it is the most fundamental division between Jews and Arabs. Whatever specific event may spark a particular confrontation, it all comes back to the basic issue of the land. On the one hand, Jews believe their rights to ownership of the land go back to their original covenant with God, while on the other hand the Palestinian Arabs point to the many centuries in which they have occupied this same territory. It is, of course, beyond the remit of this particular book to delve deeply into this most difficult of political situations – that would take a book in its own right. Suffice to say that at the time of writing in 2009, wars and *intifadas* may come and go but the underlying conflict about land still remains unresolved and will remain so until someone discovers the key to making possible the two state solution and the sharing of the land.

A HISTORICAL PERSPECTIVE

Human beings have inhabited this area for at least 4000 years. The earliest evidence of settlement has been found at Jericho and dates from about 2000 BC, but it is believed the city was already several thousand years old at that time. Civilization built upon civilisation can be seen at a glance in several 'tels' or earth mounds which have been cut through by archaeologists in such places as Jericho itself, and Megiddo. There follows a selected list of dates of the main events.

BC

2000–1500	The Biblical patriarchs.
1400	Exodus to Egypt. Pharaoh Tutankhamun.
1300–1200	The law giving at Mt Sinai. Moses and Joshua. Israelite invasion of Canaan. Fall of Jericho.
1200–1030	Period of Judges – Samson, Samuel, Saul.
1030–933	Saul, David and Solomon. The first Temple at Jerusalem.
933–722	Divided Kingdoms of Israel and Judah. Elijah and Elisha. The call of Isaiah. Samaria taken by the Assyrians, and Jerusalem besieged.
700–600	Jeremiah. Babylonian Empire.
587	Jerusalem and Judah fall to Nebuchadnezzar. Jerusalem destroyed.
587–424	Exile in Babylon. The exiles return. Second Temple built. The restoration.
332	Persians defeated by Alexander the Great.
323	Death of Alexander. Rule of Ptolemies.
198	Palestine passes from Egyptian to Syrian rule.
167	Maccabaean revolt.
141	Independence under the Hasmoneans.
63	Roman occupation begins.
37–4 AD	Herod the Great. Third Temple.

AD	Jesus of Nazareth
10	Tiberius is Emperor.
20-30	Jesus' baptism and preaching. His death and resurrection.
30-40	Conversion of Paul. Caligula. King Herod Agrippa I.
40-50	Paul's first missionary journeys. Roman conquest of Britain begins.
50-60	Paul's letters and third journey. Emperor Nero. Death of Paul.
70	Titus quells revolt of the Jews, Romans destroy the Temple.
73	Final stand of Jewish patriots at Masada.
135	Hadrian puts down revolt by Bar Kochba. Jerusalem rebuilt as Aelia Capitolina.
334	Christianity becomes official religion of Rome.
614-629	Persian occupation.
636-1099	Islamic occupation.
1099	First Crusade. Jerusalem taken.
1291	Fall of Acre, end of Crusader period.
1254-1516	Rule of Moslem Mamelukes.
1516-1917	Ottoman-Turkish rule.
1917	The Balfour Declaration.
1922-1948	British Mandate.
1947	Dead Sea Scrolls found at Qumran.
1948	Declaration of Independence, followed by war between Arabs and Jews.
1949	Armistice, and division of Jerusalem.
1956	Campaign in Sinai. Suez Crisis.
1963	Excavations at Masada under Yigael Yadin.
1967	Six-Day War. Israel 'reunites' Jerusalem and occupies West Bank.
1973	October war as Arab states attack Israel, ceasefire arranged after five weeks fighting.
1993	Peace accord between Israel and Palestinians.
1994	Israel and Jordan sign Peace Treaty.

Part 2
IN AND AROUND JERUSALEM

TOPOGRAPHY

Jerusalem is marked by a number of hills (or Mounts) and three deep valleys, though the passage of time and the amount of building has somewhat flattened the perspective, unless you stand on one of the higher vantage points.

The Old City stands some 2600 ft above sea level on two spurs which extend south-east from the main watershed. It is defined by the Hinnom Valley to the west and south, and the Kidron Valley to the east, running below the Mount of Olives and Mt. Scopus. The Tyropean Valley is now hardly traceable as it is within the present walls and almost completely silted up. It started near the Damascus Gate and ran towards the Kidron in a southerly direction. There was almost certainly another depression running east-west from the present St. Stephen's Gate to the Jaffa Gate, naturally dividing the city into four areas which are still known and occupied as the Jewish, Armenian, Moslem and Christian Quarters.

Of the hills the western spur is Mount Zion, while the eastern one is Ophel, which linked with Mt. Moriah. Both Zion and Ophel are outside the present walls but, as we shall see, were within the city at the time of Jesus.

THE WALLS

The siting of the original city of David was for a long time a matter of some conjecture. It might have been on Mt. Ophel or even Mt. Zion. It is now generally agreed that the original city was built round the Gihon Spring, the city's water source, on a south-eastern hill to the south (left) of the Temple Mount when viewed from the Mt. of Olives. On the east it borders the deep Kidron Valley, site of the Spring. It was only in the time of Solomon that the city limits expanded beyond the south-eastern spur. Subsequently rulers such as Hezekiah, Jonathan Maccabeus and Herod the Great all played a part, to a greater or lesser extent, in building, fortifying and restoring the city walls. In terms of size New Testament Jerusalem was not much different from the present day Old City, but a little further south. Old Testament Jerusalem, however, was a great deal smaller.

The most important factors which relate to the time of Christ are:

(a) Herod the Great fortified the two walls on the more vulnerable north with the three towers of Hippicus, Phasaelus and Antonia.
(b) These two northern walls were both to the south of the present northern boundary, so that the site of Calvary, the present day Church of the Holy Sepulchre, would then have been outside the walls.
(c) The southern wall was further south than the present one so that Mt. Zion, with the Dormition Abbey and the Cenaculum, was then inside the city.

Later, Agrippa (AD 41-44) built a third wall even further north, but this and the second wall were breached by Titus before his final assault on the city and the fall of Jerusalem to the Romans in AD 70. Hadrian finally obliterated what remained and built the Roman City of Aelia Capitolina in about AD 135. The present walls were built by Sultan Suleiman the Magnificent in AD 1542 during the Ottoman occupation of the city, and in doing so he probably used the foundations of Hadrian's city.

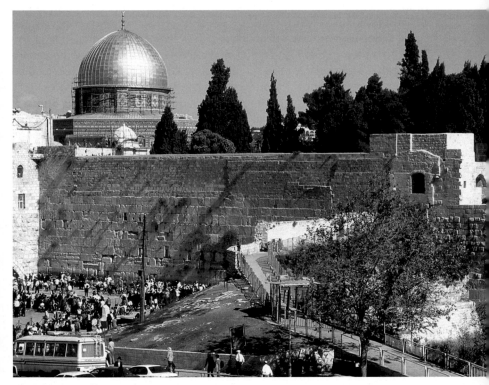

The Western Wall

OUTSIDE THE WALLS

THE KIDRON VALLEY, as already mentioned, runs below the Old City Walls and divides them from the Mount of Olives opposite. Jesus would have crossed the Valley on Palm Sunday and entered the city in the area of what is now the walled up Golden Gate, but which in those days was known as the Eastern Gate and was adjacent to the Temple and its courtyards. When David fled the city after the revolt led by Absalom (II Sam. 15:23) he crossed the brook of Kidron and wept as he climbed the Mount of Olives on his way to the Jordan (II Sam. 15:30). The Kidron is sometimes referred to as the Valley of Jehosaphat, containing the so-called **Tombs of the Prophets** and where, according to Biblical tradition, God will judge the nations of the earth. The east side of the valley contains a number of such tombs, some of which are given popular names which in point of fact have nothing to do with historical reality. One such impressive edifice with the conical roof is known as the Tomb of Absolom, son of David, but is now dated to the second part of the first century BC, and another is the Tomb of Zechariah, one of the twelve Minor Prophets, distinguished by its pyramid-shaped roof and dated to the latter part of the second century BC.

The **Gihon Spring**, is a little way along the valley, close to where it joins the Tyropean Valley. In 1867 an Englishman called Charles Warren discovered a 43 ft shaft leading up from this spring and by lowering buckets water could be drawn up from the spring without venturing outside the city walls – particularly useful in time of siege. The shaft, now popularly known as **Warren's Shaft**, is dated to about the 10th century BC. It may well have been the means by which David captured the city from the Jebusites (II Sam. 5:8). As already mentioned this was probably the site of the original city of David and its original water supply. Here also are **Hezekiah's Tunnel** and the **Pool of Siloam**. Siloam means 'sent', possibly because the water was diverted from Gihon by Hezekiah as a defence against Sennacherib (II Kings 20:22). The tunnel, some 1700 ft in length, took the water from the Spring to a large new storage pool, the Pool of Siloam, and was discovered accidentally by an Arab boy. An inscription describing the construction of the tunnel was found on a rock close to the entrance to the Pool, which as well as its Old Testament association was also mentioned in the healing of the blind man by Jesus (John 9:1-7). Visitors can wade through the tunnel from the Gihon Spring, though often in thigh-high water, but make sure you wear something on your feet and carry a torch!

Just to the south-west of the Old City is **Mount Zion**. Its major landmark is the **Dormition Abbey**, a Benedictine foundation consecrated in 1906 to commemorate Mary's death, or falling into an 'eternal sleep'. It is a beautiful building with excellent modern mosaics presented by many nations and built over an earlier Byzantine church, which was regarded as the 'Mother of all

Churches' because tradition declared this to be where the Last Supper was held and where the Holy Spirit was received by the disciples. Adjacent to here is the **Cenacle** or **Upper Room**, originally part of the Byzantine church just mentioned, in which there is an opportunity to reflect on the Last Supper and Pentecost. The vaulted room we now see probably goes back no further than Crusader times in the 13th century and the arches are typically Gothic. Later it became a mosque as evidenced by the mihrab and an Arabic inscription. In fairness it should be pointed out that the Syrian Church of St. Mark in the Old City also lays claim to being the Upper Room. A few steps away is the reputed **Tomb of David**, a Jewish holy place, but in spite of being a highly revered site among Jews its authenticity is doubtful as 1 Kings 2:10 refers to David being buried on the eastern hill. There is also a small Holocaust museum.

Not far from here is the **Church of St. Peter Gallicantu**, the 'Church of the Cock Crowing', completed in 1931 and beautifully restored in the 1990s. Regarded by some as the house of the high priest Caiaphas, it stands on the steep eastern slope of Mt. Zion with commanding views across the Kidron Valley to the Mount of Olives, as well as to Mt. Ophel, and is therefore a good point from which to understand the geography of the area. Excavations have revealed a prison and a lower pit, and if not the actual prison in which Jesus was held, then certainly they are a powerful visual aid. In terms of Peter weeping at his betrayal of Jesus it is much more likely that the High Priest's house was nearer the top of the hill among the wealthy. While you are here also notice the ancient Hasmonean stairs which once linked the top of the hill with the rest of the city and which may well have been used by Jesus and his disciples.

THE MOUNT OF OLIVES

Taking the road up the hill from Kidron you pass between the **Mount of Olives** on your right and **Mt. Scopus** to the left. This is marked by the original Hebrew University (during the division of the city this was in Arab hands and a new one was built in the modern city). At the top of the hill is a British war cemetery, close to the Augusta Victoria Hospital. Turning right at the top of the hill we see a major landmark, the tower of the Russian Church of the Ascension. This is the highest point in Jerusalem and also marks the site of the Ascension of Christ, according to the Orthodox tradition. There is a remarkable view to the left as the land sweeps down as desert and on a good day the Dead Sea, some 15 miles away, is clearly visible.

We come first to the **Chapel of the Ascension**, a modest stone structure built on a rock within the grounds of a small mosque. A small circular chapel was built by the Byzantines in the 4th century and the Crusaders replaced this with an octagonal one, also constructing a fortified monastery. It then became a mosque and has remained as such ever since because Moslems also revere the Ascension of Jesus.

Next on our journey is the **Church of Pater Noster**, dating from the 19th century but standing on the site of a 4th century church built under the direction of Queen Helena, but later destroyed by the Persians. Unlike the other Gospel tradition placing the Lord's Prayer during the Galilean ministry, Luke associates it with Jesus' time in and around Jerusalem, and so this particular church has become associated with the Lord's Prayer. As you walk around the cloisters you will see the Prayer displayed on coloured ceramic tiles in more than 70 languages. From here a road leads down to **Bethphage**, the traditional starting point of Jesus' entry into Jerusalem on Palm Sunday, a route still much used by pilgrims.

The **Observation Point** in front of the Seven Arches Hotel is the stopping point for most groups and also a possible opportunity for a group photo! This has to be one of the world's most famous panoramic views and is particularly striking in the morning light. Across the Kidron Valley is the Temple Area, dominated by the golden Dome of the Rock and to its left the grey dome of the El Aksa Mosque. The whole eastern spread of the walls can be seen, along with the walled up Golden Gate and to the right of that the St. Stephen's (or Lion)

The Ancient and the Modern

Gate. The Jewish cemeteries on the Mount of Olives mark this as an area to be particularly revered as many Jews wish to be buried here so that they are close to the Valley of Jehosphat (Kidron), where it is said that human beings will be resurrected on the Day of Judgement.

So, using your imagination, it is possible to reconstruct from here the events of Palm Sunday and Holy Week. The procession from Bethphage, over the hill behind us, winds its way up the hill and down the other slope. In a few minutes we will see the Church of Dominus Flevit where, according to Luke, Jesus wept over the city and then further down the hill Gethsemane, where he was betrayed. Then up towards the Temple Area via the Golden Gate, also known by its Greek name, the Beautiful Gate – the gate through which Jews believe the Messiah will enter the city from the Mount of Olives and the gate which is said to have been walled up by Suleiman to prevent such an eventuality! Looking further into the distance you can see the grey dome of the Church of the Holy Sepulchre, culmination of the Way of the Cross. Looking even further into the distance you can see some of the high-rise buildings of the new city, notably the David Tower of the YMCA which appears behind the square block of the King David Hotel.

Now let us follow the Palm Sunday road on foot. We come first to **Dominus Flevit** ('The Lord Wept' – Luke 19:41–42), a lovely little church designed in the shape of a teardrop by the Italian architect Antonio Barluzzi and built in 1955 over the site of an earlier 7th century Byzantine Church. Its famous window behind the altar, with its motifs of chalice and thorns, frames a wonderful view of the Old City and not unnaturally is a much-photographed scene, especially in the morning sun. Continuing downhill we pass the golden-domed Russian Church of **St. Mary Magdalene**, built in the 19th century on the order of Tsar Alexander III. There are only two narrow opportunities in the week for visitors, on Tuesday and Thursday mornings.

At the foot of the hill is the **Garden of Gethsemane** and the adjacent **Church of All Nations**, also known as the Church of the Agony. The garden is beautifully and lovingly tended by the Franciscans and contains some extremely old olive trees, though it is unlikely that the ones we now see were there in the time of Christ. As their trunks do not have rings it is impossible to date them with any precision, but some may be a thousand years old or even more. The garden has been filled with cacti, bougainvillea and oleander. When I first visited the Garden in 1971 you could walk anywhere along the paths between the flowers and trees, but nowadays visitors are channelled around the perimeter. If you want to hold devotions here, much the best thing is to arrange with the guardian to go into the garden and facilities provided on the other side of the lane from where you entered. It is usually much more peaceful there and an offering is appreciated. The word Gethsemane is from the Hebrew *Gat Shemen*, meaning 'olive press'. The church was built in 1924

The Old City

and is another Barluzzi design, its darkness capturing the mood of Christ's time in the Garden. Financial gifts from 12 nations are marked by the 12 cupolas, and the Rock of Agony inside is surrounded by a crown of thorns in wrought metal. In the floor glass plates show fragments of mosaic flooring which remain from an earlier church.

Several caves in the area are believed by different traditions to have associations with the life and death of Christ. One, the Franciscan Grotto of Gethsemane, may have been where Jesus gathered with his disciples and was betrayed. Another, known as the Tomb of Mary, leads down through a Crusader archway to the Church of the Assumption, which in the Orthodox tradition is where Mary was buried and then 'assumed into Heaven', though the Dormition Abbey is more popularly venerated.

A practical word of warning though – in the holy city unholy things happen, so please beware of the pickpockets who can be around this area.

THE OLD CITY – CHRISTIAN SITES AND THE VIA DOLOROSA

For our tour we shall enter the Old City by the St. Stephen's Gate on the eastern side, which faces the Mount of Olives, so that we can follow from here the Way of the Cross, or Via Dolorosa, and then separately visit the Temple Area, the Western Wall and the various quarters of the city. It is also known as the Lions Gate, because of the heraldic lions set on either side of the gate by Suleiman's architects.

We come first, on the right hand side, to the **Church of St. Anne**, a superb example of pure Crusader architecture and possessor of a wonderful acoustic, especially for singing. Most groups appreciate an opportunity to sing here – 20 people singing can sound like a choral society of 200! But please don't stay too long - other groups want to do the same. It is reputed to be the home of Mary and her parents, Joachim and Anne. Having at one time been turned into a Moslem seminary, it was beautifully restored in the 19th century. Adjoining the Church are the **Pools of Bethesda**, which the followers of Asclepius, the Roman god of healing, believed to be medicinal baths providing healing. Built originally in the 8th century and known as 'the upper pool', it ran south and helped to supply water to the City of David. It is now widely understood to be where Jesus healed the man who had waited thirty-eight years for someone to help him down into the healing waters (John 5:1–15). The excavations have uncovered steps, porches and paving, as well as the remains of a Roman Temple and a later Byzantine church, and illustrate how far below the present street level was the Jerusalem which Jesus knew and walked.

A short distance further along the street is the Franciscan **Chapel of the Flagellation**, commemorating the scourging of Jesus by the Roman soldiers, and at the other end of the courtyard is the **Chapel of the Condemnation**. Opposite here is the Umariyya School from where the Friday procession of the 'Stations of the Cross' begins, though there is now strong scholarly opinion that Jesus' trial and condemnation took place not here at the Antonia Fortress, but rather at the Citadel, from where the Via Dolorosa would have started. However, this area still remains an evocative location in which to commemorate these significant events. The nearby **Convent of the Sisters of Sion** is built on the site of the Antonia Fortress, the massive Roman garrison guarding the Temple from the north at the time of Jesus, and which Herod the Great dedicated to Mark Anthony. Here you can see the remains of the Struthion Pool, an ancient reservoir which collected rainwater from the rooftops. Also to be viewed is a stretch of pavement, often referred to as the *Lithostrotos*, and which some believe is that mentioned in John 19:13, but there is strong archaeological evidence that the pavement is more likely to be 2nd century rather than 1st. Also in the convent is a railed off area in which you can see, marked into the stone, the kind of game which Roman soldiers may well have played and has become identified as the King's Game. The **Ecce Homo Arch**, which is actually half of a Roman triumphal arch, was built by Hadrian in 135 AD, and marks the words of Pilate presenting Jesus to the people, 'Behold the Man'. This marks *Station II*.

STATIONS OF THE CROSS
At 3pm each Friday a Franciscan procession leads pilgrims along this traditional Way of Sorrows, bearing a cross. All are welcome to follow.

I	Jesus is condemned to death (Mt 27:26-31)
II	Jesus receives His Cross (Jn 19:17)
III	Jesus falls the first time (Traditional)
IV	Jesus meets His mother (Traditional)
V	The cross is laid upon Simon of Cyrene (Mk 15:21)
VI	Veronica wipes the face of Jesus (Traditional)
VII	Jesus falls the second time (Traditional)
VIII	Jesus speaks to the women of Jerusalem (Lk 23:27-31)
IX	Jesus falls a third time (traditional)

The remaining stations are within the Church of the Holy Sepulchre:

X	Jesus is stripped of His garments (Jn 19:23)
XI	He is nailed to the cross (Lk 23:33)
XII	Jesus dies upon the cross (Mk 15:37)
XIII	The body of Jesus is laid in the arms of His mother (Traditional)
XIV	His body is laid in the Sepulchre (Mt 27:59-60)

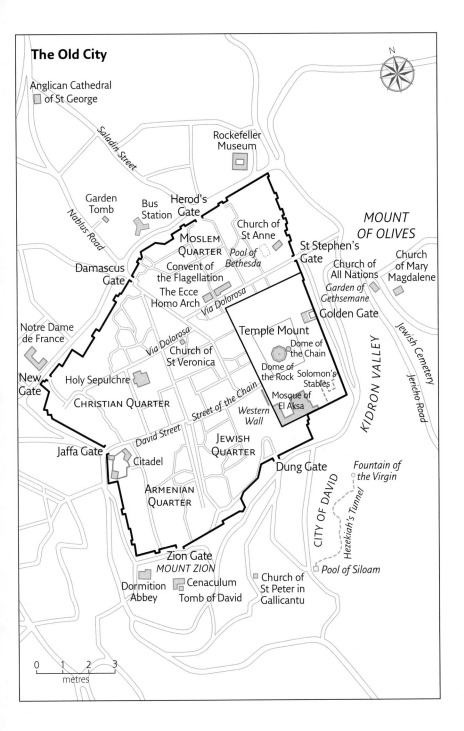

The Old City

N

Anglican Cathedral
of St George

Saladin Street

Rockefeller
Museum

Garden
Tomb

Nablus Road

Bus
Station

Herod's
Gate

Church of
St Anne

MOSLEM
QUARTER

*Pool of
Bethesda*

St Stephen's
Gate

MOUNT
OF OLIVES

Damascus
Gate

Convent of
the Flagellation

Church
of Mary
Magdalene

Church of
All Nations

*Garden of
Gethsemane*

The Ecce
Homo Arch

Via Dolorosa

Golden Gate

Notre Dame
de France

Via Dolorosa

Church of
St Veronica

Temple Mount

Dome of
the Chain

JEWISH CEMETERY

New
Gate

Holy Sepulchre

Dome of
the Rock

Solomon's
Stables

Jericho Road

CHRISTIAN QUARTER

Street of the Chain

Mosque of
El Aksa

Jaffa Gate

David Street

JEWISH
QUARTER

*Western
Wall*

KIDRON VALLEY

Citadel

Dung Gate

Fountain of
the Virgin

ARMENIAN
QUARTER

CITY OF DAVID

Hezekiah's Tunnel

Zion Gate

MOUNT ZION

Dormition
Abbey

Cenaculum

Tomb of David

Church of
St Peter in
Gallicantu

Pool of Siloam

0   1   2   3
métres

Before progressing any further along the **Via Dolorosa** it should be pointed out that this is more a route of religious faith than historical reality and, indeed, the route has changed over the centuries. That, however, does not prevent it being a powerful medium of devotion. I realise that there are some Protestants who will find this particular style of devotion foreign to the spirituality they have experienced, particularly as Stations 3, 4, 6, 7 and 9 are not based on any Biblical evidence. However, as an open mind is crucial in any visit to the Holy Land, hopefully this will not deter them from sharing a way of prayer and devotion which other Christians find meaningful.

So, continuing on our way, we follow the road downhill, turn left and on the left is a small Polish Chapel, with a stone relief, marking the place where Jesus falls for the first time (*Station III*). Just further along here, on the same side, is *Station IV*, (Jesus meets his mother). Turning right the Via Dolorosa climbs uphill and we find the next *Station (V)*, where the cross is taken up by Simon of Cyrene. About halfway up is the Church of St. Veronica, the woman who wipes the face of Jesus and finds the imprint of his face left on the cloth (*Station VI*). At the top of the hill we meet a street leading to the Damascus Gate and here is *Station VII*, where Jesus falls the second time under the weight of the cross. Remember that today all the Stations are within the walled city, but at that time the walls were different and the place of Crucifixion was outside the city walls.

If at this intersection we turn left then immediately right, a short distance up here, opposite the shops, we find *Station VIII*, another cross on the walls commemorating Jesus speaking to the women of Jerusalem (Luke 23:27-31). Retracing our steps to the intersection and then turning right takes us through the crowded Suk or market. A short way along here is a stone stairway on the right, and climbing this brings us to *Station IX*, a pillar embedded in the wall by the Coptic Patriarchate, where Jesus falls the third time.

The remaining stations are within the **Church of the Holy Sepulchre** itself, which can be accessed by continuing through the Ethiopian quarter on the roof and then descending through two small chapels to emerge in the courtyard in front of the main doors. In 325 AD the then Bishop of Jerusalem, Makarios, asked permission of the Roman Emperor Constantine to demolish the Temple of Aphrodite and unearth the Tomb of Christ said to be buried beneath it. The rock tomb was eventually discovered in this ancient quarry and the surrounding rock was cut away to create the shrine known as the Anastasis or Resurrection. Also revealed nearby was a rocky hill which was identified with Golgotha, the place of the Crucifixion. Constantine then authorised the building of a Basilica to incorporate both Golgotha and the Tomb, and in 326 his mother, the devout Queen Helena, visited the site. Far removed though it may be from the picture of 'a green hill far away', if you go down into the depths of the church you can begin to see the way in which it was built on a hillside as you observe various caves, and the evidence points to this being, in all probability, the place of the final climactic events of Christ's ministry. It is known, too, that burial chambers existed here in the first centuries BC and AD. The Basilica built by Constantine was later set on fire by the Persians in 614 AD and then systematically destroyed in the 11th century by the Arabs. Soon rebuilt on a smaller scale by a Byzantine Emperor in that same century, it was significantly enlarged by the Crusaders in the 12th. But a fire in 1808 and an earthquake in 1927 caused further considerable damage and it was not until 1959 that the three major communities (Latins, Greeks and Armenians) came to an agreement about the the Basilica's repair and renovation, the fruits of which can now be observed. It follows no uniform architectural pattern, but has been fashioned through history and argument with many a bitter dispute among the various sects now laying claim to it, the Syrians, Copts and Ethiopians in addition to the three just mentioned.

To the contemporary pilgrim it is a place which can inspire and infuriate, delight and disappoint in equal measure. We look for harmony, tolerance and sanctity and yet too often find discord, division and frailty. A church which points to glory all too often exposes human weakness. And yet, in spite of all the contradictions, it draws people in droves. Though seen by many as the personification of the divisions within Christianity, yet nonetheless it remains the holiest of holy sites and central to the beliefs of every Christian.

Station X (Jesus is stripped of his garments) is located just inside the main door. A narrow (and steep!) stone stairway takes us up first to the Franciscan Chapel on the right, marking Jesus being nailed to the Cross (*Station XI*). On the left of this is the Greek Orthodox Chapel (*Station XII*), Jesus dies on the Cross. Pilgrims may reach under the altar to put a hand through the hole and touch the top of the rock in which the Cross is said to have been set. Returning to the lower level we find the Stone of Unction, or Anointing, (*Station XIII*), where his body is taken from the Cross and prepared for burial, before being interred in the Holy Sepulchre itself (*Station XIV*). The tomb donated by Joseph of Arimathea would have been a two-roomed crypt cut into the rock. Much of it has now disappeared and the rest is covered in marble and other decoration. Only about six people can enter the tomb at a time.

Within the rest of the church are many small chapels dedicated to different events and by different traditions. The Greek Orthodox Katholikon has a spot which claims to be the Centre of the Earth. The Franciscan chapel of Mary Magdalene is where Mary discovered the resurrection of Jesus. Behind the High Altar steps lead down to the Chapel of Helena, now in possession of the Armenians, and further stairs on the right lead down to where Helena is reputed to have discovered the true cross, though this is a highly dubious tradition.

On leaving the courtyard of the Holy Sepulchre, a left turn will bring you to the Lutheran **Church of the Redeemer**, with its tower which dominates the skyline, but if you turn right it is just a short walk to the **Jaffa Gate**, the busiest of the Old City gates. In this area is the Anglican Christ Church, which also has a Guest House.

THE TEMPLE AREA – MOSLEM AND JEWISH SHRINES

The **Jaffa Gate** is a good place to commence our second walk inside the Old City, this time to look at mainly Moslem and Jewish sites. The Gate itself consists of a pair of massive towers forming part of the **Citadel of David**. This contains the Jerusalem Municipal Museum and is the site for *son et lumière* performances in the summer. Originally attributed to David, when this was thought to have been the Palace of David, it is now believed that this was a mistaken identification by the Byzantines. The towers to fortify the city were in fact built by Herod the Great and the site was used as a fortress by Romans and Crusaders and later added to by Suleiman the Magnificent. Leading straight ahead into the bazaars is David Street, and almost as a continuation of this is Chain Street which brings us to the **Temple Mount**. Half way along, however, is a crossroads within the bazaar at which a left turn will bring you to the Damascus Gate and so ensure that you have seen the major shopping area of the Old City.

The flat, walled-in plateau of the Temple Mount was both the site of the First Temple, that of Saul, David and Solomon, and also the Second, which was known to Jesus. Having been destroyed in 586 BC by the Babylonian invasion, the First Temple was replaced by the Second Temple 70 years later. Eventually Herod the Great sought to ingratiate himself with his Jewish subjects and embarked on an ambitious building programme for the Temple which made it one of the most imposing structures in the ancient world. The present area covers some 34 acres and without doubt its major landmark is the **Dome of the Rock**. Set over Mount Moriah this is an area sacred to Jews, Christians and Moslems, for as well as being where Abraham prepared to slay Isaac, it is also where Moslems believe that Mohammed ascended to heaven after his night journey to Jerusalem. For Jews, so sacred is this area that they will not enter this upper part of the Mount for fear of treading on the Holy of Holies. A magnificent octagonal structure, topped by a golden-dome and with walls of beautiful coloured tiles, some of which contain inscriptions from the Quran, it was built in 685 AD by the then Caliph of Damascus. There are four entrances (at which you must leave your shoes) and inside are 56 beautiful windows, with two concentric rows of marble pillars supporting the ambulatory and the inner dome. Roof and walls are gold, with mosaics in all colours, and the floor is covered with Persian carpets. At the centre is the rock where Abraham

The Dome of the Rock

prepared to sacrifice Isaac. Moslems say that Mohammed's footprint is embedded in it, and in a grotto below they believe kings and prophets came to pray. The rock is surrounded by an intricately carved wooden screen. Since the start of the second *intifada* on 28 September 2000 (ended February 2005), it has not been possible for pilgrims/visitors to enter the Dome, so it can only be hoped that this will change at some point.

The other major building on the Temple site is the **El Aksa Mosque**, built in a style in complete contrast to the Dome of the Rock. This today is the leading place for Moslem prayers each Friday and its vast, open area can hold thousands. It is supported by 45 great columns, the painted arabesque ceiling and the lovely stained glass windows (all 121 of them) giving an air of opulence. The magnificent pulpit and beautiful carpets add the final touches. Between the two mosques is Al Kas (The Cup), a circular fountain for ritual ablutions before prayers and dating from 1320.

The smaller **Dome of the Chain** is a miniature copy of the Dome of the Rock and is supported by 17 columns; there is an ornate little kiosk of Mameluke design and a summer pulpit to be used for outdoor prayers. The legend behind its name is that it once had a chain suspended from the roof and whoever told a lie while holding the chain would be struck dead by lightning.

Leaving the upper plateau of the Temple Area you return to the lower level at the **Western Wall** (or Wailing Wall) of the Temple. Most sacred of Jewish sites, this was part of the western retaining wall of the Second Temple destroyed in 70 AD and is virtually all that remains of it. For that reason it has for centuries been the custom for Jews to weep over the destruction of the Temple. But as well as praying at the Wall, worshippers place prayers on scraps of paper into the cracks between the stones. The larger stones at the lower levels are certainly Herodian and from the time of the Second Temple period, those above were added later. Whatever time of day or night you come here you will find people praying, though as in an Orthodox synagogue there is strict segregation of the sexes. Non-Jewish men may approach the Wall as long as they cover their heads and dress appropriately. On Shabbat and the great Jewish Festivals you will find many hundreds of people gathered. Also not to be missed, if the opportunity presents itself, is to be here for the Bar or Bat Mitzvahs, the religious coming of age ceremony for a boy or girl. These are held on Monday and Thursday mornings.

A visit to the **Western Wall Tunnel** should be a high priority, though tours/visits have to be reserved in advance, and it is not for the claustrophobic! Excavations uncovered a labyrinth of tunnels, arches and passageways which had been undiscovered for centuries. In visiting the tunnel you are walking along a street in Jerusalem during the Herodian/Second Temple period. This runs north along the outside face of the Wall, exposing its foundations, and along here, too, are the remains of a Hasmonean water channel. The whole experience is a fascinating walk through history as you tread the same way used by countless pilgrims in Second Temple times.

Before leaving this area one further visit is recommended and that is to the **Ophel Excavations**, an attractively laid out space on the southern side of the Temple Mount and just inside the Dung Gate (so-called because of refuse being taken out from the city through this gate). You can walk along streets and view the remains of shops, stalls, ritual baths, cisterns and residential houses. In addition you can see and climb the original monumental staircase (though a good deal has been reconstructed) allowing entrance and exit through the gates that led into the Temple. These are the Hulda Gates, the eastern one is triple-arched and the western one double, in all probability at times of great Jewish Festivals one being used as an entrance and the other as an exit. There can be little doubt that these steps would have been used by Jesus and his disciples.

Behind the spacious plaza which now fronts the Western Wall is the area known as the **Jewish Quarter**, a largely residential area. This has been the subject of much sympathetic rebuilding since the re-unification of Jerusalem. It includes a centre for writers and artists and there are many galleries, studios and craft shops. It is a locality best visited on a Saturday evening at the end of

Shabbat when it is full of life. There are, of course, many synagogues, including the Ramban, the oldest still standing and dating back some 700 years, a centre of prayer and Torah learning. Next door to it is the Hurva Yehuda He-Hasid Synagogue, formerly the centre of Ashkenazi worship, and though destroyed in the Arab-Israeli conflict of 1948 rebuilding is finally due to be completed during 2009. But one of the most important pieces of archaeological work has been the re-discovery and restoration of the **Cardo Maximus** originally laid by the Romans, and which in Byzantine times became Jerusalem's main thoroughfare. What we see today is the Byzantine extension of the Cardo, and its importance is demonstrated by the way in which it appears in the 6th century AD Madaba Map in Jordan, a mosaic depicting Jerusalem at that time. The **Armenian Quarter** adjoins the Jewish one and takes in all of the south-eastern part of the walled city as far as the Jaffa Gate. Particularly noteworthy is the **Cathedral of St. James**, a most beautiful building dating back to the 11th and 12th centuries and considerably renovated since. If you have the opportunity to join their daily service it is an experience not to be forgotten. The **Christian Quarter** we have already visited, since it centres around the Holy Sepulchre, and similarly the **Moslem Quarter**, occupying the north-west sector, has within it the Church of St. Anne and the first part of the Via Dolorosa. But most pilgrims will want to explore the area for the atmosphere and aromas of the Bazaars which line many side alleys as well as the two main streets which meet just before the **Damacus Gate**. This is the grandest of the city gates, being the major pedestrian access and leading out to the area known as East Jerusalem. The present gate was built in the 16th century by Suleiman the Magnificent, though excavations have revealed part of the earlier structure going back to Roman times, probably those of Agrippa (41–44 AD).

THE EVENTS OF HOLY WEEK

A VIEW FROM THE ST. STEPHEN'S GATE

We are standing with our backs to the city walls and looking towards the Mount of Olives. The Feast of Passover is drawing near. The city is crowded and thousands of pilgrims are encamped in the surrounding hills and valleys.

Palm Sunday Crowds are moving up the Mount of Olives to greet Jesus, who has left Bethany for the little village of Bethphage, out of sight behind the hill. He rides on the donkey, and those surrounding him wave their palm branches with the greeting, 'Hosanna'. Jesus stops, surveys the City from the hillside and weeps over Jerusalem (Church of Dominus Flevit). He continues down the hill, passing the Garden of Gethsemane, to which he will return later in the week, and crosses the Kidron before riding up the hill and entering the city. Read: Mt. 21:1–11, Mk. 11:1–11, Lk. 19:29–44, Jn. 12:12–19. On the first day Jesus looks over the Temple and returns to Bethany.

Monday   Today, Jesus returns to Jerusalem and entering the Temple he drives out the traders and money changers from the outer court of the Temple, the Court of the Gentiles. This is regarded as such a threat to the Temple system and its economy that the final conflict with the authorities becomes inevitable. He then returns to Bethany. Read: Mt. 21:12-16, Mk.11:12-19, Lk. 19:45-48.

Tuesday   Jesus spends the day teaching and discussing in the Temple. He speaks of the Wicked Husbandmen, the Tribute Money and the Widow's Mite. Once again he spends the night in Bethany. Read: Mt. 21:23-22:40, Mk. 11:27-12:44, Lk. 20:1-21:4.

Wednesday Jesus teaches on the Mount of Olives, while across the valley the Sanhedrin plot his death and conspire with Judas. He speaks in parables about the Day of Judgement and predicts the destruction of Jerusalem. Read: Mt. 24:1-26:16, Mk. 13:1-14:11, Lk. 21:24-22:6.

Maundy Thursday   In the evening Jesus and the disciples celebrate the Passover in the large Upper Room. After this they visit the Garden of Gethsemane, an olive grove at the foot of the hill. Read: Mt: 26:17-56, Mk. 14:12-50, Lk. 22:7-51, Jn 13:1-18:10. But the solitude of Gethsemane is broken by the tumult of voices and the flaming torches of the conspirators. Judas then betrays his master with a kiss. The Sanhedrin is hastily summoned to the house of Caiaphas, the high priest, probably somewhere in the region of St. Peter in Gallicantu, and Jesus is condemned by them.

Good Friday   In the morning he is taken to Pilate, who hopes that Jesus will be released by the will of the people, but they choose Barabbas instead. Jesus is sentenced to death and commences the long walk to Golgotha (the Church of the Holy Sepulchre). Read: Mt. 26:57-27:29, Mk. 14:53-15:15, Lk. 22:54-23:25, Jn. 18:12-19:16.

EXPLORING EAST JERUSALEM

East Jerusalem is that part of town which, prior to 1967, was in Jordanian hands and as a result is populated mainly by Arabs. The Damascus Gate is its focal point and standing with our backs to it, the roar of traffic, the peddlers, beggars and animals leave us in no doubt that we are in an oriental part of the city. Looking to the right the road follows the line of the walls before dipping down into the Kidron Valley. The main post office stands at the foot of Saladin Street, the main shopping and business area, and the large building at the top of the hill is the **Rockefeller Museum**, which has one of the major archaeological collections.

Straight ahead of us is the Nablus Road, and a short distance up here a lane on the right leads to the **Garden Tomb**. It was discovered in 1883 by General Charles Gordon who, not being overly impressed with the Holy Sepulchre, thought that this location fitted in well with that of Calvary, though most scholarly opinion dismisses the site in favour of the Holy Sepulchre. Nonetheless, it is well worth a visit for, correct location or not, the Garden Tomb has the surroundings and ambience which readily recreate those which would have prevailed at the time. It is an excellent visual aid, for what it lacks in authenticity it makes up for in atmosphere. The tomb itself has a burial chamber and rolling stone set into a groove. Above it is a hill which has the visible markings of a skull, Golgotha, and the whole area is beautifully and lovingly tended by an organisation based in England. There are several places around the Garden where groups may conduct their own services and facilities are provided for Holy Communion.

Further up the road is a junction just before coming to the **East Jerusalem YMCA**. Behind this is an open space where once stood the Mandelbaum Gate, the only crossing place between east and west in the days of Partition. The YMCA has its own story to tell, for it was born out of the 1948 partition when thousands of homeless Arabs found themselves in huge refugee camps in the Jericho area. The YMCA started as a vocational training centre, which still exists, and in addition now has a Rehabilitation Centre for those who are physically challenged and traumatised.

Further on is the **Anglican Cathedral of St. George**, the seat of the Bishop of Jerusalem of the Episcopal Church in Jerusalem and the Middle East. Looking just like an English parish church it has a guest house and a college which conducts short term and longer term courses for clergy and laity of the Anglican Communion. There is a Palestinian service at 9.30 a.m. (with translation!), which gives an opportunity to meet some of the local Palestinian Christian community, and then there is an English service at 11.00 a.m.

Beyond here are the so-called Tombs of the Kings. First excavated in 1863, they were attributed to the Kings of Judah, but later work has shown them to be at least 1st century AD, possibly belonging to Queen Helena of Adiabene in Mesopotamia.

WEST JERUSALEM

The western (or Jewish) part of the city is not far away from the Old City Walls in distance, but the contrast in styles is striking. Turning left out of the Damascus Gate and following the street alongside the walls brings us to the New Gate at the north-west corner. Turn right at the traffic lights and this brings you to **Jaffa (Yafo) Road**, the major spinal artery of the western city. This leads eventually to **Zion Square** (Kikka Ziyyon), from which the pedestrianised **Ben Yehuda Street**, with its shops, pavement cafes and continental atmosphere, provides the focal point of all things modern. It, too, is worth experiencing on a Saturday night at the end of Shabbat. You may have walked little more than half a mile but you have travelled from one world to another. **King George V Street**, at the top of Ben Yehuda, is another major traffic route. On it are many of the Jewish religious centres, including the Jerusalem Great Synagogue.

Further out from the centre, on the outskirts of the city, are several places of interest. The splendid **Israel Museum** built in 1965 has various magnificent collections of art and sculpture arranged in a modern and attractive setting. The Bronfman Archaeological Museum illustrates various periods of Israel's history (including discoveries from Masada), and the Bezalel Museum demonstrates Jewish life throughout the centuries. But the majority of pilgrims may have time for only two of the exhibits here. The first is the **Shrine of the Book**, built to display the finds in and around Qumran. The construction resembles the lid of the jars in which the Dead Sea Scrolls were discovered by an Arab boy in 1947. The air-conditioned, sunken building shows the complete 23 ft scroll of Isaiah dating from the 1st century BC and entirely visible in one particular case. This is usually a copy to preserve the condition of the original, which very occasionally is put on public display. Other texts from Qumran are also displayed along with objects found in nearby caves. The scale **Model of Jerusalem** at the time of the Second Temple, i.e. at the time of Jesus, which used to be displayed at the Holyland Hotel, was recently removed and re-sited at the Israel Museum. Clearly a good deal of imagination, in addition to evidence, has been used in constructing this impressively large site. Yet the model gives an excellent idea of the city as it might have been and particularly the Temple itself, enabling the viewer to put into some perspective the various sites visited – a most helpful visual aid in fitting Jerusalem together.

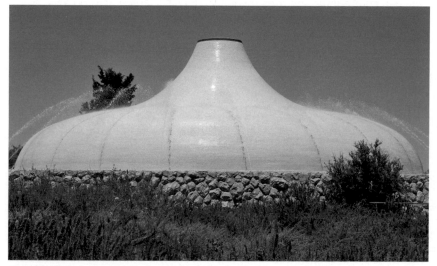

The Shrine of the Book

In the same area is the Israeli Parliament Building, the **Knesset**. An attractive, modern building, it is open to the public on certain days and has some fine stained glass windows by Marc Chagall. At the entrance is a huge Menorah, the seven-branched candlestick which is Israel's symbol. This was presented by the British Parliament. Also in this part of the city is **Mount Herzl**, named after Theodor Herzl, the Austro-Hungarian writer, who became the first president of the World Zionist Organisation and one of the founders of the eventual State of Israel. His tomb is here along with those of other later leaders such as Levi Eshkol, Golda Meir and Yitzak Rabin. Not far away is the Holocaust Museum at Yad Vashem, the terrifying but effectively impressive tribute to the millions of Jews killed by the Nazis. Approached along the Avenue of the Righteous, there are a number of memorials to be seen, including the Hall of Remembrance, with its eternal flame, and perhaps most moving of all, the Children's Memorial, dedicated to the estimated 1.5 million children who were exterminated. Opened in recent years is the new **Holocaust Museum** of History. A visit to Yad Vashem is a most sobering and moving experience.

Westward from this point the road divides, the upper one going to the **Haddasah Hospital**, whose small synagogue contains a series of windows commissioned from Marc Chagall to depict each of the Twelve tribes of Israel. The lower road leads to **Ein Kerem**, situated in a very picturesque area, with tradition declaring that this was where John the Baptist was born and lived, the home of his parents Zechariah and Elizabeth, and the site of the meeting between Mary and Elizabeth. There are two particular churches here – one is the **Church of St. John the Baptist**, with the earliest church on the site going back to the 5th century, followed by later Byzantine and Crusader ones, and the other is a two level church, **The Church of the Visitation**, first begun in 1938 and completed in 1955 from a design by Barluzzi. Not surprisingly the courtyard walls are lined with tiles on which are inscribed the words of the *Magnificat* in more than 40 languages. As the village was visited by Mary there is also a spring named for her (the Spring of the Virgin).

Elsewhere in the western part of Jerusalem are some other places worthy of note. The YMCA in King David Street has a fine chapel and a tower, known as the David Tower, which is one of the landmarks of the city. Standing opposite is the King David Hotel, one of the city's most opulent and often used by statesmen. Not far away is **Montefiore's Windmill**. In the early 19th century Sir Moses Montefiore found a great number of Jews living in poverty, so he built the windmill for them to grind corn, together with a residential quarter. **St. Andrew's Church** of the Church of Scotland on Abu Tor also has a welcoming guest house. The Scottish King, Robert the Bruce, wanted his heart to be buried in Jerusalem but his wish went unfulfilled, though there is a plaque in the floor of the church to commemorate him (Sunday service at 10.00 a.m.).

Bethlehem – The Church of the Nativity

Part 3
JOURNEYS FROM JERUSALEM

BETHLEHEM - HEBRON - HERODION

About five miles from Jerusalem in a southerly direction is **BETHLEHEM**, now controlled by the Palestinian Authority, so passports are essential as in effect you are crossing a border from Israeli controlled territory into Palestinian. The history of the town goes back as far as the 14th century BC though it only really comes into prominence with the birth of David, whose great-grandparents, Ruth and Boaz, also lived here.

As you arrive at Bethlehem and just before you cross the control zone, you will see on the right a tomb known as **Rachel's Tomb**. Though quite an ancient tradition lies behind this being the actual location, there is reason to believe it may be mistaken. Once through the check-point the coach will take you to a large parking area and then you must walk up into Manger Square for the visit to the **Church of the Nativity**. As with the Church of the Holy Sepulchre, this area was identified for Queen Helena as the setting for Christ's birth. As a result, in 326 AD Constantine ordered the building of the first church here and this was dedicated by Helena in 339. The present building dates back to the time of the Emperor Justinian, who had it rebuilt in about 530, and though re-decorated by the Crusaders and given its fortress-like appearance, the basic structure of the Church today remains much the same. Entrance is through a low doorway, requiring the pilgrim to stoop low on entry, and was designed in this way to stop people riding into the church on horseback. The oak ceiling goes back to the 14th century, a gift from Edward III of England, and beneath trap doors in the floor can be seen ancient mosaics from the original 4th century church. Custody is divided between the Armenian, Greek Orthodox and Roman Catholic churches. Marble steps lead down to the **Grotto of the Nativity** which marks the birthplace of Jesus. The cave of the nativity is one of a number of such caves in the area and the silver 14-pointed star in the floor is said to mark the place of birth.

The Catholic **Church of St. Catherine** is dedicated to one of the earliest pilgrims and martyrs who came from Alexandria and who paid for her faith in a spectacular death by fire – the lights inside the church reproduce the effect of the Catherine Wheel. Built by Franciscans in the 1880s it is on the site of earlier churches, the first being a 5th century monastery associated with St. Jerome. On the right-hand side of the nave are steps which lead down to more caves under the Church of the Nativity and it is possible to hold a group devotion here. In the courtyard is a statue of **St. Jerome** (c. 340–420) who, as well as establishing a monastery in Bethlehem, also produced the first Latin translation (the Vulgate) of the earlier Greek texts.

Back outside there are wonderful views across the fields from the terrace at the side of St. Catherine's and all pilgrims will want to go down to **Beit Sahour** and the region of the **Shepherds' Fields**, where there are both Orthodox and Roman sites. In all probability the caves around here were used by shepherds and the Franciscan cave in particular is most useful for an act of worship.

A visit to the Holy Land also provides an opportunity to meet up with 'living stones' and to visit and share in the work of some of the charitable organisations here. One such possibility is the ***Bethlehem Arab Society for Rehabilitation***. Founded originally in 1960 as one of the Leonard Cheshire homes it is a non-profit, non-government organisation nationally recognised for the comprehensive medical and rehabilitation services available to people from different parts of Palestine, particularly those with special needs. All this is offered irrespective of gender, age, religion or social standing. Its mission is to improve the quality of life of the Palestinian population, particularly those with disabilities. It is possible for a group to book lunch here and to be shown around, and the Society readily accepts gifts of bedding, towels, toys, etc., which members of groups bring with them. This, however, is but one of a number of 'living stones' projects which may be visited but it is one which the author knows particularly well.

HEBRON is less often visited these days than it used to be because of the difficult relationship there between Jew and Arab. It has a long history of war, persecution and slaughter, even up to more recent times. A cauldron of Palestinian political life it has always had a minority Jewish Quarter whose population lives in uneasy cohabitation with the Arab majority and from time to time this breaks out into open hostility. Nevertheless, it is an important place in Biblical history, for nearby is the site of ancient Mamre, one of the oldest continuously inhabited places on earth. Here lived Abraham, Sarah, Isaac, Rebecca, Jacob and Leah, all of whose tombs can be seen. Here the promise was made to Abraham and Sarah of the birth of Isaac (Gen. 18). It later became the capital of the powerful tribe of Judah and David reigned here for seven and a half years (II Sam. 5:5) before transferring to Jerusalem as King of Israel. The huge **Tomb of the Patriarchs** is largely based on a Crusader construction but later became a mosque, and both Jews and Moslems use the place for prayer. Hebron is also famous for its beautiful coloured glassware.

HERODION is a conical shaped volcanic mountain, a few miles south-east from Bethlehem, and from a distance appears to have had its top lopped off. Herod built a fortress at the summit and a settlement below. He used it as one of his summer palaces and for very many years one of the great unsolved archaeological mysteries was whether or not he was buried here. But in May 2007 Prof. Ehud Netzer, an archaeologist from the Hebrew University, announced that Herod's tomb and mausoleum had indeed been discovered and continuing work seems to confirm this. Excavations have revealed many of Herodion's features, including watch towers, storerooms and reservoirs, plus a mosaic floor from a later, Byzantine period.

EMMAUS AND BETHANY

These are two separate journeys since they lie on opposite sides of Jerusalem. In practice each will be visited on different excursions with other places, but because of their importance they deserve a brief section to themselves.

BETHANY (Arab name – El Azariya) is a small village on the eastern side of Jerusalem on one of the roads towards Jericho, though it is hidden from the city by the Mount of Olives. Here was the occasion of the Raising of Lazarus (Jn. 11:1–44) and where he was a frequent visitor to the home of Mary, Martha and Lazarus (Lk. 10:38–42, Jn. 12:1–8). This was also where Jesus stayed with Simon the leper (Mk. 14:3–9). A new Franciscan church was built in 1953 over the traditional site of the home of Mary and Martha. According to Jerome there was a church on this spot in 390 and in the courtyard of the present building you can see masonry from that church. Once inside, colourful mosaics depict the incidents related in Luke 10 and John 11. The entrance to the **Tomb of Lazarus** is up a small lane from here and some uneven steps take you down into the tomb, though there is room only for a few people at a time. If you continue up the lane you come to Bethphage and then from there up to the top of the Mount of Olives.

While there is little problem about identifying Bethany, the same cannot be said when it comes to **EMMAUS**, where after his Resurrection Jesus made himself known to Cleopas and another disciple. At least four places lay claim to being Emmaus, though only three are normally visited. The problem is one of distance, as there is some doubt as to whether it lay 60 or 160 stadia (i.e. 7 or 18 miles) from Jerusalem. One site is at **Abu Ghosh** on the road from Jerusalem towards Tel Aviv and this fits with the 60 stadia marker as suggested in Luke's Gospel (Lk. 24:13–31). Authentic or not there is a lovely Crusader church kept by the French Benedictines. Some way further along the same road is another site at **Amwas (Imwas)**, close to the Monastery at Latrun. Although it has the oldest tradition identifying it as Emmaus, the distance of 160 stadia raises serious doubts. There is also a Crusader church.

The most often shown site is that at **Qubeiba**, in the Judean hills just north of Jerusalem, and since about 1500 has been the place most popularly associated with Emmaus. There was a Crusader settlement here and the present Franciscan church has an impressive fresco showing the two Disciples eating with Jesus. There is a tradition that the church was built over an earlier church which in turn was built over the ruins of an ancient room, now venerated by many as the house of Cleopas. But again there are doubts about authenticity.

In the first century AD there was another Emmaus somewhat closer to Jerusalem, about 4 miles, and was eventually known by the name **Qoloniya**. While it could fit in with Luke's story that the two disciples walked there and back on the same day as the Resurrection, that is about all that can be said in its favour. So all in all, identifying Emmaus remains a somewhat inconclusive exercise!

SOUTH TO BEERSHEBA AND EILAT

The most popular and direct route from Jerusalem to the modern tourist resort of Eilat on the Red Sea follows the coastal road along the Dead Sea from Jericho, but those interested in the history and Biblical significance of the journey will want to travel via Hebron and Beersheba for a real feel of the Negev, the vast desert which covers almost four thousand square miles.

BEERSHEBA is often referred to as the Capital of the Negev and in recent decades its population has been boosted by immigrants from Ethiopia and the former Soviet Union. It boasts the famous University of the Negev, founded by David Ben-Gurion, and now known as the Ben-Gurion University of the Negev. There are also centres for medical, pharmaceutical and desert research. Still very much a Bedouin city, one of its special attractions is the Thursday Bedouin market.

But its history is immense, this 'City of the Patriarchs', where Abimelech, king of Gerar, made Covenants with both Abraham and Isaac (Gen. 21:32, 26:33); where Elijah fled from Jezebel before his journey into the wilderness (1 Kings 19:3) and where Jacob made sacrifices. Archaeological excavations have revealed traces of life from the 4th millennium BC. Among the chief points of interest today are the seven famous wells, one of which is known as Abraham's Well. Just outside the city is **Tel Beersheba**, where David built a fortified town. There are remains here of a city gate, a Roman fortress and a large horned altar, the original of which is in the Israel Museum.

Travelling due south we come first to **Sde Boker**, where David Ben-Gurion made his home from retirement until his death, and where his home and library can be visited. Almost the whole town is a shrine to his memory. The road in this region provides spectacular scenery, climbing steep mountains and

The Mount of Olives with (bottom left) the Church of All Nations

diving into deep wadis such as **Ain Avdat**, which has a pool and luxuriant growth at its foot. **Avdat** itself was a Nabatean centre (they who ruled Petra) and has the remains of a Byzantine Monastery. **Mitzpe Ramon** sits on the edge of a sheer 900 ft precipice overlooking a crater six miles wide and 25 miles long. **Timna** is a copper mining town, the oldest excavations being popularly known as King Solomon's Mines, though archaeologists have established that they were Egyptian and operated in the Bronze Age and Iron Age. In this area are a number of mining operations which produce the attractive green grained mineral known as Eilat Stone, which features in much of the costume jewellery sold throughout Israel.

We finally arrive at **EILAT**, mentioned in the Bible as Eloth and important during the kingdoms of Judah and Israel. Today it is chiefly known as the resort centre of Israel's 7 mile stretch of Red Sea coast, a holiday destination in its own right and popular for winter sun breaks, with a huge selection of ultra modern hotels and amenities. There are very good beaches and facilities for water sports and scuba diving. The spectacular coral reefs with a myriad of brightly coloured fish can also be seen from a trip on a glass-bottomed boat or at the underwater observatory on the edge of town.

Eilat, however, is also a good centre for touring into neighbouring countries with, for example, the opportunity of crossing to the Jordanian port of Aqaba only a few miles away. A visit to Petra can be made as a day trip from here, as also can Mount Sinai and St. Catherine's Monastery in Egypt, though both trips will be much more comfortable and rewarding if done in at least two days.

THE DEAD SEA - MASADA - QUMRAN

This is a full day tour made available to most pilgrimage groups, even though there is little of purely Biblical significance within it. Yet that apart, it will remain a particularly memorable day. Soon after leaving the boundary of Jerusalem you are immersed in desert and you will be fascinated by the rock formations, the variety of colour and structure to be found on either side of the road. Deep wadis (dried up river beds) attract the nomadic Bedouin with their sheep and goats but, arid as they may appear, they can be the occasion of dangerous flash floods which carry sudden forces of water down from the wilderness to the Dead Sea. At one point on the road your guide may well point out the **Good Samaritan Inn**, forgetting that this was only a parable! It is the ruin of an old khan, or inn, but the surrounding landscape brings to life the circumstances of that story (Lk. 10:30-37). Some way further on a sign tells us that we have reached sea level and by the time we are at the foot of the hills and coming along the shores of the Dead Sea we shall be at the lowest point on earth, roughly 1300 ft below sea level.

The **Dead Sea** is about 50 miles long and approximately 11 miles wide at its maximum, though there is some discrepancy in the figures depending which authority you read! The reason for this uncertainty is the dramatic annual shrinkage of the Sea due to extremely high levels of evaporation, plus the fact that both Israel and Jordan take water out of the Jordan river for agriculture and industrial purposes. As a result not enough water flows into the Sea to top up the level. However, there is a strong possibility that a canal may be built from the Red Sea to the Dead Sea. The water has a very high saline and mineral

Floating in the Dead Sea

Masada – a view from the summit

content and the extraction of salt, potash and other minerals is a major industry at the southern end. Furthermore, the mud from the Dead Sea is highly thought of in both health and beauty treatments. There are several sulphur springs along the shore and if you visit one of the spas to experience 'floating' in the Sea, then you will probably also have an opportunity of bathing in the springs, though on a tour it is usual to do this after first of all ascending **Masada**.

The summit of Masada stands some 1300 ft above the level of the Dead Sea and is reached either by cable car or, for the energetic, by a tortuous route known as the Snake Path. This was the site of a fortress well before the time of Christ, but later developed by Herod the Great who built not one but two palaces here. During the Jewish revolt against the Romans it was in the hands of the zealots, and in 70 AD those who survived the destruction of Jerusalem fled south for refuge at Masada. The traditional story is that for three years, under the leadership of Eleazar ben Jair, they held out against the might of the Roman Tenth Legion. When finally the Romans took it, by building a ramp on the western slope and then setting fire to the wooden fortifications, they discovered that 960 men, women and children had chosen death with honour rather than surrender their freedom and be taken into slavery. It is said that two women and five children hid while this happened and so later they were able to recount the events. The story was written up by the Jewish historian, Josephus, who later transferred his allegiance to Rome and became a Roman citizen, but it has to be said that there are those who have doubts as to the reliability of his account. Maybe only time and further research will unearth the truth. But for all that, it is a visit not to be missed.

Full-scale excavations began in 1963 under Professor Yigael Yadin (who later became a member of the Israeli Government). The remains of palaces, store-rooms, bath houses, a synagogue, a Byzantine church and water storage systems have all been uncovered and in part reconstructed, but not so as to appear phoney. The huge range of finds included coins, scroll fragments and pottery, and the 'cannon ball' stones which were used to repel the Romans can also be seen. In addition you can look down on to the assault ramp as well as the outlines of the Roman camps. An audio-visual presentation and restaurant are available.

To the north of Masada along the Dead Sea coast is the oasis of **Ein Gedi**, where a kibbutz guest house and restaurant provide facilities for bathing in the buoyant waters. But better still is the Health Spa a short distance away where there are sulphur baths and private access to the Dead Sea. But if there is time a walk inland brings you to a lush oasis where abundant animal, including ibex, and bird life can be observed. Mentioned in the Bible for its beauty it is also the place where David is said to have taken refuge from King Saul.

Returning towards Jerusalem is **Qumran**, where in 1947 a shepherd boy looking for a stray goat accidentally found jars containing the precious

The cave at Qumran where the Dead Sea Scrolls were found

parchments now known as the ***Dead Sea Scrolls***. They seem to have been hidden in caves by a community believed to be Essenes, who occupied this area from about 150 BC until they were expelled by the Romans in 68 AD. It may even have been the Biblical City of Salt mentioned in Josh. 15:62. Thought to have been written between the 3rd century BC and 68 AD the scrolls contained various Biblical texts, including some of the oldest ever found, as well as accounts of their daily life and their rule book. Since their discovery the Scrolls have created much ongoing academic and theological debate about their significance. Before visiting the archaeological site where, among other things, some of the caves can be seen, there is a helpful audio-visual presentation.

NORTH TO GALILEE VIA THE WEST BANK AND SAMARIA

This is a route not much commonly favoured by tour companies in recent years as it runs through territory which now mostly forms part of the Palestinian Authority area. That doesn't mean, however, that it is out of the question. It was occupied by Israel from 1967 and its two main towns, Ramallah and Nablus, have often been centres of unrest. But it does have a number of places of Biblical interest. In all probabilty it would have been the route taken by Joseph and Mary to and from Jerusalem, and so would have been known to Jesus. Taking the Nablus road from the Damascus Gate we come after about four miles to Tel El-Ful, where Albright discovered the walls and turrets of a fortification, probably the first royal castle of Gibeah where Saul reigned. To the right of the road is Ramah, where Samuel was born, lived and died (1 Sam. 7:17). Here, David fleeing from the jealous anger of Saul, sought the protection of Samuel (1 Samuel 19:9-18).

Fleeing from Beersheba, Jacob rested at Luz, 12 miles from Jerusalem, and saw a vision of a ladder. He named the place **Bethel** (Gen. 28:11-19). In the days of the Judges, the Ark of the Covenant rested here and the shrine of Bethel rivalled that of the Temple, but it was later condemned. As we approach Shilo there is a wonderful view to the right of the **Valley of the Dancers**. The tribe of Benjamin, still loyal to the House of Saul, were shunned by the other tribes but an arrangement was made by which they took wives from the maidens who danced at the religious festival at Shilo (Judges 21).

At **Shilo**, probably on the high knoll to the right, stood the Temple where Eli was priest, served by the boy Samuel. Because the Ark of the Covenant rested here it became an important sanctuary, probably destroyed by the Philistines (Jer. 7:12 & 14). Approaching Nablus we call first at **Jacob's Well**, venerated as the place where Jesus met the woman of Samaria (Jn. 4:4-42). Jacob bought a piece of land and erected an altar (Gen. 33:18-20). His daughter, Dinah, was raped and avenged by her brothers, Simeon and Levi, who destroyed the city. **Shechem**, as Nablus was called, was an Israelite city of refuge, once walled, but has been continuously occupied since the Bronze Age. When the Romans rebuilt it they called it Flavia Neapolis, the Arabic translation of which is Nablus. The Crusaders also occupied it in 1099. The nearby **Mt. Gerizim** is sacred to Samaritans – Alexander the Great permitted them to build a temple on it. According to Joshua 8:33 it was used by Joshua when pronouncing the Law. The Samaritan temple was destroyed by Hyrcanus in 432 BC and Vespasian slaughtered some 11,000 Samaritans. There is a long history of bitterness between the Samaritans and Jews and few of them remain today, though they have a modern temple in Nablus and still celebrate their Passover on Mt. Gerizim.

We are now in Samaria, and we find at Shomeron the site of **Sebastiya**, once the capital of the Kingdom of Israel from the 9th century BC. It is said that Ahab built a temple on this site in honour of Baal, under the influence of his wife, Jezebel, and for his blasphemy the prophets foretold that Sebastiya would become a heap of stones. The Roman Emperor Augustus presented the city to Herod who considerably enlarged and renovated it. According to legend this was where Salome danced for the head of John the Baptist, whose tomb is claimed to be here. The remains on view today result from a series of 20th century excavations and include ruins from the earliest Kings of Israel as well as from Herodian, Byzantine and Crusader times, but mostly they are from the Roman era with a great amphitheatre, hippodrome and temple.

Some 14 miles further north is the city of **Dothan**, where Joseph was sold by his brothers and taken to Egypt (Gen. 37:17) and where an attempt was made to capture Elisha (II Kings 6:13). Finally we come to Jenin, ancient Engannin where, according to tradition, Jesus cured the ten lepers, and then we cross into Galilee.

WHAT IS A TEL?

The prefix Tel will often be found to place names in Israel. It refers to an artificial mound, usually eliptical in shape, which has been formed over many centuries by the accumulated residue of settlements which have been built, then abandoned or ravaged by war, built up again, destroyed, re-built and so on. Many are unexcavated, but those which have been, by archaeologists cutting a wide and deep trench through the centre, have produced evidence of many civilisations, one on top of the other. The most important such sites in Israel are those at Megiddo, Jericho, Beit She'an, and the largest at Hazor in Northern Galilee. In the Arabic version the word is spelled Tell.

Some other place names and prefixes you will come across (Arabic version in parentheses):
Bet (Beit) = House   Rosh (Ras) = Summit
Kefar (Kafr) = Village   Beier (Bir) = Well

NORTH TO GALILEE VIA JERICHO AND THE JORDAN VALLEY

This more commonly used route follows the same road from Jerusalem as for the Dead Sea and Masada excursion, but before the final stage of the descent to the plain it is well worth taking a small side road to the left which brings you to the gorge known as **Wadi Kelt**. This provides a stunning view of the **Monastery of St. George**, a Greek Orthodox establishment carved out of the sheer rock wall leading down into the ravine. Founded in the 5th century it was destroyed by the Persians in 614 and later partially rebuilt by the Crusaders, being more completely restored in the 19th century. It can be visited by arrangement and hardy pilgrims sometimes walk to it from Jerusalem or Jericho. Remains of mosaics from the 6th century can still be seen. Stopping in this area also helps to give a feel of the wilderness and a short time of silence to soak up the view and the atmosphere is a most worth-while experience. It also helps to set the scene for the story of the Temptations of Jesus.

The first sighting of **Jericho** from high above gives a fine impression of what an oasis is all about. Its lush fields and orchards stand out starkly from the surrounding desert and provide an abundance of fruit and vegetables which supply not only the population of the Palestinian Authority area, of which Jericho is a major centre, but are also exported across the Allenby Bridge into Jordan. The best way to experience the stark contrast is to take the cable car up to what is known as the **Mount of Temptation**, riddled with caves and topped with a monastery, a reminder of that inner conflict through which Jesus went after his Baptism as he sought to discover the style of Messiahship he ought to follow. From the cable-car station at the top there are magnificent views of the surrounding area illustrating the contrast between the arid and the fertile. It is a good place to enjoy a coffee while soaking up the panorama!

Jericho itself has long claimed to be the oldest inhabited city on earth, though these claims are now disputed by archaeological finds elsewhere. Excavations date it back to 9000 BC and it is certainly the world's lowest city. It was the Canaanite Jericho which fell to Joshua (Josh. 6:20, 24) in about 1200 BC and was the first place he conquered after crossing the Jordan. Its waters were purified by Elisha (II Kings 2:19–22) and Pompey encamped here. Anthony gave it to Cleopatra, who in turn leased it to Herod. With that kind of history how could it not be a fascinating place to visit? And indeed it is – the deep cut made through the Tel by the well-known British archaeologist Kathleen Kenyon shows how the various civilisations were built one on top of the other. One of the most impressive remains to be seen is the stout tower of a gateway dating back to 7,000 BC. Jesus visited Jericho a number of times, including his encounter with the tax-collector, Zaccheus, (Lk. 19:1–10), and the healing of the two blind men (Mt. 20:29–34).

From here we continue north along the Jordan valley to visit the town of **Beit She'an**, a fine example of a Roman-Byzantine town, and in the time of Jesus one of the cities of the Decapolis. This is where the Philistines displayed the bodies of Saul and his sons on the walls. Conquered by King David it then became one of the main centres of Solomon's rule. There is much worth seeing – the theatre, the baths, the nymphaeum, the main street, a temple, a basilica, an amphitheatre – and still excavations continue. A climb to the top of the Tel by a secure stairway is much recommended as it offers a splendid overview of the city and it is believed that within the Tel are 20 layers of civilisations, piled on top of one another, from the 4th millennium BC. Certainly, a visit here is a must.

On leaving Beit She'an we soon come to the southern edge of the **Plain of Jezreel** and this allows a tour of **Megiddo**. Although it may be too much to include on the transfer day to Galilee, it may be possible to fit it in at some other point of the itinerary. This whole site is controlled by a kibbutz, which can be visited – it has a restaurant and makes and sells jewellery. From Pharaoh Thutmose III in the 15th century BC to General Allenby, from the victory of Deborah and Barak (Judges 5) to the final battle of Armageddon (Rev. 16:16), the strategic importance of Megiddo has been recognised. The excavation of the great Tel shows at least 20 layers of culture, from 4000 BC downwards, including Canaanite temples, Egyptian and Hebrew seals, Solomon's Chariot City, Ahab's Stables, a sunken silo, a primitive flour mill, and the famous Megiddo ivories. Megiddo is not only the gateway to the Galilee, it is the gateway to the whole Middle East. The span and significance of its history is breathtaking, and the walk through the subterranean tunnel which formed its water system will not easily be forgotten.

St George's Monastery at Wadi Kelt

Part 4
THE GALILEE

LOWER GALILEE

Galilee begins with the Plain of Jezreel (Ah Emek Yesreel), along the southern border of which we travelled in the last chapter to reach Megiddo. This triangular valley is known as Israel's breadbasket, as it is the most fertile and productive in the country. It was not always so for, in Biblical times, and even until it was purchased by the Jewish National Fund in 1921, it was a pestilential swamp, a fact which played some part in the turbulent history of the area.

To the south are the Samaritan Hills, including the Carmel range; to the north are the mountains of lower Galilee, beginning at Nazareth, whilst to the east is an irregular range of hills which include Mount Tabor, one of two possible sites for the Transfiguration of Christ, Mt. Moreh (or little Hermon), Mt. Gilboa and the intervening valleys. The three bastions of Carmel, Tabor and Gilboa, together with Megiddo at the Wadi Ara Pass, have played a formidable part in shaping the history of this region. The Israelites under Deborah and Barak, inferior in numbers and equipment, waited on Mt. Tabor until the Plain was in flood and so routed the Canaanites at Megiddo (Judges 5). Gideon, at the spring of Ein Harod, near Gilboa, chose his 300 men and defeated the Midianites (Judges 7:1-23). King Saul called on the witch of Endor (near Tabor) on the eve of battle, and was killed by the Philistines at Gilboa (1 Samuel 31). Ahab and Jezebel held court at Jezreel; and the prophet Elijah, after his epic struggle on Mt. Carmel, ran the whole length of the valley to Jezreel in front of Ahab's chariot (1 Kings 18:20-46).

The Plain has echoed with the deeds of Alexander, Pompey and Vespasian, the Crusaders, Saladin and Napoleon. Now it is the area of several renowned kibbutzim, many fish farms and market gardens. All roads converge on the market town of **Afula**, which has been suggested as the possible location for the Biblical city of Ophel (II Kings 5:24). At any rate the town represents the real gateway to the Galilee and offers two possible roads to the Sea of Galilee.

The eastern road leads past Nain, where Jesus raised the widow's son (Luke 7:11-15), to **Mount Tabor**, one of at least two possible sites for the experience of the Transfiguration, the other main contender being Mt. Hermon in the

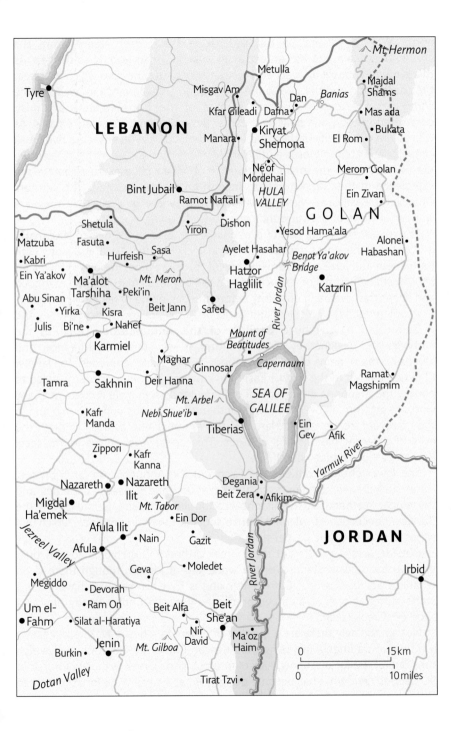

Tyre

LEBANON

Metulla
Misgav Am
Kfar Gileadi Dafna
Manara Kiryat
Shemona
Dan Banias
Majdal
Shams
Mas ada
Bukata
El Rom
Merom Golan

Bint Jubail
Ramot Naftali
Ne'of
Mordehai
HULA
VALLEY

Ein Zivan

GOLAN

Shetula
Matzuba
Fasuta
Kabri
Hurfeish
Yiron
Dishon
Sasa
Yesod Hama'ala

Ayelet Hasahar
Hatzor
Haglilit
Benot Ya'akov
Bridge

Alonei
Habashan

Ein Ya'akov
Abu Sinan
Ma'alot
Tarshiha
Peki'in
Mt. Meron
Yirka
Kisra
Beit Jann
Safed
Katzrin

River Jordan

Julis Bi'ne Nahef
Karmiel

Mount of
Beatitudes
Capernaum

Maghar
Ginnosar
Tamra
Sakhnin
Deir Hanna
Kafr
Manda
Mt. Arbel
Nebi Shue'ib
Tiberias

SEA OF
GALILEE

Ramat
Magshimim

Ein
Gev
Afik

Zippori
Kafr
Kanna

Nazareth Nazareth
Ilit
Mt. Tabor

Degania
Beit Zera Afikim

Yarmuk River

Migdal
Ha'emek
Afula Ilit
Nain
Ein Dor
Gazit

JORDAN

Jezreel Valley
Afula
Geva
Moledet

River Jordan

Irbid

Megiddo
Um el-
Fahm
Devorah
Ram On
Silat al-Haratiya
Beit Alfa
Beit
She'an
Nir
David
Ma'oz
Haim

Jenin
Mt. Gilboa

Burkin
Dotan Valley
Tirat Tzvi

Mt Hermon

0   15 km
0   10 miles

north. With its distinctive rounded shape Tabor rises steeply from the surrounding Plain and has an extremely winding road leading to the top. As this is not negotiable by coaches it is necessary to use the taxis which wait near the coach park, and the ride to the top is quite an experience in itself. On the summit is the lovely Franciscan Basilica of the Transfiguration of Christ, completed in 1924 and built over earlier Byzantine and Crusader remains. As well as the main body of the church, on either side as you enter are two small chapels dedicated to Moses and Elijah (Read Mt. 17:1-8). Since the 4th century AD this has been the main location for Christian pilgrims to celebrate the experience of the Transfiguration, though a case can be made for Hermon. Outside the Basilica are viewing platforms from where, on a clear day, there are wonderful views of the surrounding regions of Galilee.

The road which leads north from Afula brings us over the hills to **Nazareth**. In spite of its noisiness and, at times, grid-locked traffic, Nazareth, along with Bethlehem and Jerusalem, remains one of the three most important towns for the Christian pilgrim. For it was here that the boy Jesus matured into manhood and spent thirty years in obscurity before the beginning of his public ministry.

Populated today by Moslem and Christian Arabs, the town sits in a valley and is dominated by the huge **Basilica of the Annunciation**. Built by the Catholics and designed by Giovanni Muzio, it was consecrated in 1969, and stands on the remains of earlier Byzantine and Crusader churches. The largest Christian church in the Middle East, it is crowned by a huge lantern, styled to portray the Madonna lily, a symbol of Mary. Modern in style it contains many works of art from all over the world, both in the spacious upper church and in the courtyard, representing Mary and the Annunciation as seen through the eyes of different nations and cultures. This upper level serves as the local Roman Catholic parish church.

The lower church contains the Grotto of the Annunciation (Lk. 1:26-38). Here can be seen remains from the Byzantine and Crusader churches and these help to emphasise the historical continuity of the site. Before leaving the Basilica, notice also its splendid bronze doors at the main entrance, which in a series of reliefs tell the gospel story.

Outside, across a courtyard, is the Greek Orthodox Church of St. Joseph, built in 1914 and said to stand over the workshop of Joseph, though there is no reliable tradition for this. Current thinking is that he may well have been a stone-cutter as well as a carpenter, for the gospels simply identify him as a 'worker' (Greek *tekton*).

Not surprisingly there are a number of other churches in Nazareth, kept by a variety of traditions, including the Anglican Church of Christ Church, which runs one of the local schools. Also of interest is the Greek Orthodox Church of St. Gabriel, near what has become designated as Mary's Well, for according to Orthodox tradition the annunciation took place while Mary was drawing water

Nazareth – Basilica of the Annunciation

from the well. It is a delightful little church and well worth a visit. Some groups also appreciate a visit to the Synagogue Church, commemorating the site of Jesus worshipping and preaching in the synagogue, but no evidence has so far been found to support any claim to authenticity. For all that, however, it is still an excellent place for an act of devotion.

A more recently established project is the **Nazareth Village**, the result of archaeological and academic research, which has constructed a farm and a Galilean village – Nazareth as it might have been in the time of Jesus. A useful educational experience and visual aid, it contains such features as a wine press, stone quarry, well, olive press, workshop, sheepfold and synagogue. Many pilgrims find it a helpful introduction to life in first-century Galilee. It is also possible to organise a first-century meal.

A few miles north of Nazareth is the small Arab village of **Cana** (Kafr Kanna), visited by pilgrims as the traditional place where Jesus attended the wedding feast and turned the water into wine (Jn. 2:1-11). There are three main commemorative churches, one of which is claimed to be the site of Nathaniel's house, though the majority of visitors seem to head for the red-domed Franciscan Church, often referred to as the 'Wedding Church'. It should be pointed out that there is no unanimity of agreement that this village is the original Cana, as at least three other possible locations have been suggested.

If time permits a detour to **Zippori** (Sepphoris) has much to commend it. Capital of Galilee in Herodian times, Christian tradition declares it to be the birthplace of St. Anne, mother of Mary and, therefore, possibly of Mary herself. As it took no part in the rebellion of 66 AD it was spared by the Romans and by the second century it had become a significant centre of Jewish religious and spiritual life. In the third century the Jewish Sanhedrin was located here, though it later transferred to Tiberias, and in the fifth century it was the seat of a Christian bishopric. Remains can be seen of synagogues, public buildings and ritual baths, a temple, a theatre, a water system with aqueducts and also burial caves. Particularly noteworthy is the Mansion, with its magnificent mosaic floor, dated to the mid-third century AD with representations of scenes from the life of Dionysos, the Greek god of revelry. One mosaic is the portrait of a beautiful young woman and this has become known as the 'Mona Lisa of the Galilee'.

Returning to the main road and driving towards Tiberias, we can see the saddle-shaped mountain called the **Horns of Hattin** (or Hittin). This was where, on 4 July 1187, the Crusaders were decisively defeated by Saladin. Continuing on our journey we soon have our first view of the Sea of Galilee far below us.

AROUND THE LAKE

The Sea of Galilee – Lake Tiberias – Yam Kinneret; it has several names but derives from the Hebrew word *kinnor* or 'harp', a reference to its shape. Surrounded by hills it is 13 miles from north to south and seven miles at its maximum width. It is also 682 ft below sea level. The River Jordan enters at its most northerly point and leaves again at the southern end. Israel's only freshwater lake it supplies water to the central and southern parts of the

The "Jesus Boats" at Tiberias

country. To the east are the Golan Heights, the Biblical land of the Gadarenes (Mk. 5:1-7), rising to a plateau some 2000 ft above the lake, so that the difference in pressure between the levels can give rise to sudden and violent storms (Mt. 8:24-26), as I remember from my first visit to the area in 1971. Fishing is still an important industry and, as you can imagine, the small boats have to beware these sudden gusts.

A sail on the Lake is a 'must', especially in one of the wooden 'Jesus boats'. To go out into the Lake from Tiberias to the northern shore, for example, and for them to stop the engines so that you can experience something of the tranquility of your surroundings, is a very special experience. No group will want to miss it.

TIBERIAS is the major town, the largest on the shores of the Lake, and a popular tourist centre. Founded in the Roman period by Herod Antipas, it was dedicated to the Emperor Tiberius and became the capital of the region in place of Zippori. There is no record of Jesus having visited here, but after 70 AD it developed as a centre of Rabbinical culture and study and became one of Israel's holy cities, along with Jerusalem, Hebron and Safed. On the southern edge of the town are the Hot Springs which were certainly known to the Romans for their curative properties and are still very much in demand today, both for treatments and for the indoor and outdoor swimming pools.

Going to the southern end of the Lake brings us to where the River Jordan flows out from it and where we find the specially built Baptismal facilities at Yardenit, where many Christian pilgrims like to be baptised in the waters of the Jordan, or to renew their baptismal vows, though in all probability the Baptism of Jesus took place at Bethany beyond Jordan, on the Jordanian side of the river. Adjoining Yardenit is Kibbutz Degania Aleph, the oldest of such communal settlements, founded in 1910. The road further south follows the River Jordan and it is possible to reach the **Castle of Belvoir**, a Crusader stronghold which commands a marvellous view of the whole Jordan Valley.

The road today completely circles the Lake, but if we return to Tiberias and drive northwards we come first to **Peniel**, a lovely little chapel at the side of the road, maintained by the YMCA and which also has a hostel. Built in memory of an American who served the West Jerusalem YMCA for many years, the Harte Memorial Chapel is a simple, Gothic-shaped archway, the whole chancel end being a window with a breath-taking view of the Lake. Groups are welcome to hold services by arrangement and there is also an outdoor altar by the water's edge. Similar facilities for worship by the Lake are also available at Tabgha, Mensa Christi and, more recently, now at Capernaum.

Continuing northwards a small road leads to the Valley of the Doves, and parking the coach to take a short walk into the valley has much to recommend it for you have the feeling that you are probably on authentic ground, as this is believed to be the ancient route from Nazareth to the Sea of Galilee. Here, too, is Nebi Shue'ib, the Tomb of Jethro, a shrine which is sacred to the Druzes, and

The Synagogue, Capernaum

standing guard over the valley is Mt. Arbel, from which there are stunning views of the Lake. Almost opposite the entrance to this valley is the site of **Magdala**, the home of Mary Magdalene, which is now but a heap of stones.

Further round the northern shore and not far from Capernaum is a recently excavated site which a number of archaeologists believe to be the location of the fishing village of **Bethsaida**, though this is by no means universally agreed. According to the Gospels, Bethsaida was the home of Peter, Andrew and Philip, and maybe also James and John. Excavations have revealed a gate, street, houses (including the houses of the fisherman and the winemaker), palace and sacrificial area. It is a delightful site, beautifully located. Whether it is the actual location or not maybe doesn't matter too much!

Also in this area is Kibbutz Nof Ginosar, which has an excellent restaurant, coffee house and hotel on the lake shore. In 1986 an ancient boat was discovered half buried nearby, exposed by the lowering of the water level. It was dated between the first century BC and the first century AD, and so evidently used by fishermen at the time of Jesus. The boat is preserved in the kibbutz and can be seen.

The road climbs above the lake, passing a hydro-electric station which harnesses the waters of the Jordan as they fall from the heights of Mt. Hermon. It brings us into the northernmost part of the lake-side which played such a significant part in the ministry of Jesus. On a spur is the **Mount of Beatitudes**, another Barluzzi design and built in 1938, with some of the cost given by Mussolini. This beautiful, octagonal shaped church, symbolising the

The Mount of Beatitudes

Beatitudes, has a colonnaded portico which provides wonderful views of the Lake. In the eight walls which face the central altar are eight windows with the eight Beatitudes of the Sermon on the Mount. A gentle slope on the ridge below is sometimes suggested as the setting for such a sermon, but who knows? The whole area is beautifully landscaped and kept by the Franciscan sisters and provides an aura of peace in which to reflect on one of the very special passages from the Gospels (Mt. 5:3-10).

Returning below, back to the Lake, is **Tabgha**, where there are two important places to visit. **The Church of the Primacy of St. Peter**, or **Mensa Christi** (Table of Christ) as it is sometimes known, is built around a rock and commemorates the Risen Christ preparing a meal of fish and bread for the Disciples (John 21). It also recalls Peter's three-fold restoration after his three-fold denial of Jesus on the night of his arrest. Built in 1933 and renovated in 1984, it stands on the remains of a 4th century church, some of whose walls are still clearly visible. You can walk down to the Lake and it is a good place to spend some time on your own for reflection. Close by is the **Church of the Multiplication of the Loaves and Fishes**, which recalls the feeding of the multitude. This was dedicated in 1982 and is a reproduction of a mid-5th century church, but contains many ancient mosaics depicting the flora and fauna of the area, and most famously the 4th century mosaic of the loaves and the fishes, set in the floor in the sanctuary.

From this point it is not very far along the shore to **Capernaum**, described by Matthew (9:1) as 'his own town', which suggests that this was the nearest Jesus came to having a base in Galilee. We know that this was the home of Peter, that it was a community of about 1500 people and probably not particularly affluent. Among the buildings excavated, and partly rebuilt, is the synagogue, which according to most experts can be dated to the third or fourth century AD, though it does seem to have been built on the foundations of an earlier one, very possibly the one in which Jesus would have preached. A very modern church has been built over the ruins of St. Peter's house, and large amounts of stonework have been uncovered, some of which show rich carvings, with depictions of a Star of David, the Ark of the Covenant and the Hebrew seven-branched candlestick, the Menorah. Here, too, it is possible to walk down towards the Lake and even to use the worship areas recently created.

Driving round to the eastern side of the Lake from the northern end brings you to **Kursi**, the traditional location for the incident of the Gadarene swine. In this very attractive setting, set back from the Lake, are the ruins of a 5th century church and monastery, the largest Byzantine monastery in Israel. Further south is Kibbutz **Ein Gev** with a restaurant which specialises in the so-called St. Peter's fish and though tasty it is full of bones, but you may be able to persuade someone to fillet it for you! It is also a cultural centre with a fine concert hall.

The Church of the Primacy of St Peter

UPPER GALILEE

A tour which has good scenic value is to take a circular route from the north-eastern side of the Lake up to the Golan Heights. The road runs through a military zone, close to the present border with Syria and by-passing what is now the ghost town of Quneitra. Camps of the United Nations Forces can be seen in the distance. The object, however, is to come close to **Mount Hermon**, the highest mountain in Israel at 9200 ft, and for most of the winter and spring covered in snow, making it Israel's only ski resort. With three distinct peaks, all about the same height, it straddles the borders of Israel, Lebanon and Syria. Military outposts can be seen on two of the peaks, one Israeli, the other Syrian, each keeping a close eye on the other. Much of the Israel side is a nature reserve as well as a winter sports area. It is possible to take a chair lift to the top and this is well worth doing as I discovered on the only occasion I have so far managed. The views are truly wonderful. On the foothills of Hermon are the three separate sources of the **River Jordan** (in Hebrew – 'Yarden', the river that descends), at Senir, Banyas and Nahal Dan. The river runs for some 150 miles to the Dead Sea, over which distance it drops some 2600 ft in height. There is also an opinion that Hermon might have been a more likely location for the Transfiguration rather than Tabor, given its proximity to Caesarea Philippi and the way in which the Gospel writers link the Transfiguration with Caesarea Philippi.

The Jordan's source at Banyas, the Biblical **Caesarea Philippi**, which is mentioned both in the New Testament and the Talmud, has waterfalls and rushing streams. It is a lovely scenic area abounding with wildlife and, depending on how much time you have, there are a number of walks to enable the visitor to enjoy this delightful spot. The nearby Biblical city of **Dan** has a large and important Tel. It was the home of the Tribe of Dan and the place where Micah set up his graven image (see Judges 18:27–31). This whole region is lush with vegetation and a delight for nature lovers. Also in this area is the spectacular **Nimrod Castle** which dominates the Hula Valley. Still remaining are a number of its defensive towers along with most of its outer wall, as well as a keep and the moat.

The return journey to Tiberias is made via the town of Quiryat Shemona, but a detour could be made to the hilltop city of **Safed**, also called Zefat, one of the four 'Holy' cities of Judaism. Many brilliant Sephardim settled here after their expulsion from Spain in 1492, and later came the Ashkenazim with their culture and religious fervour. Its Synagogue Quarter, with its 16th century synagogues is not to be missed. Not surprisingly, Safed remains a major centre of Jewish learning and religion, but also of the arts. There is a vibrant Artists' Quarter with many studios, galleries and craft shops. You could spend quite a long time here!

Part 5
THE COASTAL PLAIN

The road from the Sea of Galilee to the coastal plain is little over 40 miles, with that to Acre passing over hilly country in which are several Druze villages, before descending to the plain.

Acre (Akko), the ancient walled city, has been an object of conquest throughout history. Mentioned in ancient Egyptian documents, conquered by Alexander the Great, a naval base for the Romans, and besieged but never conquered by Napoleon, its greatest days were in the times of the Crusaders, who made it their main seaport and the headquarters of the Order of St. John of Jerusalem. They named it St. Jean d'Acre and built the huge fortifications, including the enormous Crypt of St. John, an underground hall which is the best preserved Crusader church in Israel. Acre became their lifeline to Europe and they developed it as a flourishing centre of east-west trade. This was the finest period of the city's glory.

Present day Acre is characteristic of a fortified Ottoman town dating from the 18th – 19th centuries, with its sturdy defensive walls being a rebuilding of the Crusader ones. The remains of the Crusader town, dating from 1104–1291 lie almost intact, much of it below today's street level where there is an astonishing array of 12th and 13th century streets, buildings and grand halls. The Mosque of El-Jazzar, the Great Mosque, was built in Turkish style in 1781 and is the best example of Ottoman religious architecture in the Holy Land. There is also a fine example of a Caravanserai, where the camel trains from the east brought their spices and silks for sale and transhipment to the New World. In the old town the bazaar has many workshops of coppersmiths which provide the most popular souvenirs of a visit here, and the picturesque harbour is very photogenic. The Citadel stands on Crusader foundations and during the British Mandate served as a prison.

Driving south along the coastal road which skirts the bay soon brings you to the outskirts of Haifa, Israel's third city and major port, making it a flourishing industrial city. Driving up the steep slopes of **Mount Carmel** provides a stunning panoramic view of the harbour. The outstanding feature is the golden dome of the Baha'i Temple, built in Parthenon style and set in delightful Persian gardens. It is the headquarters of the Baha'i religion, which accepts a synthesis of several religions. On the western slope is the French Carmelite Monastery of Stella Maris, marking the place where the prophet Elijah had his epic struggle with the prophets of Baal (1 Kings 18:20-46). There is a lavishly decorated grotto. Mount Carmel is, in fact, a range of hills some 15 miles long and reaching a maximum height of almost 2000 ft. At its eastern extremities it forms the boundary of the Plain of Jezreel, and the northern 'finger' becomes the hills surrounding Nazareth.

From here it takes only a short time to continue down the fast road to **Caesarea**, one of the most impressive of archaeological sites. Given by the Emperor Augustus to Herod the Great, who proceeded to enlarge it in the grand manner, he called it Caesarea in honour of the Emperor. During the Roman period it was the largest city in the country, seat of the Procurator of Judea and headquarters of the Roman army. It was here in 69 AD that Vespasian was proclaimed Emperor, and Cornelius the Centurion was also stationed here (Acts 10). Paul was imprisoned at Caesarea under Felix (Acts 23:24), was tried by Festus (Acts 25:1-6) and stated his case before Agrippa (Acts 26), before sailing for Italy and Rome. The excavations have revealed a great sea port, a fortress, the impressive remains of two Roman aqueducts, a hippodrome,

The Mediterranean at Tel Aviv

marbles and mosaics from the fifth and sixth centuries, but the majority of remains are from the Crusader period. The many pieces of stonework which seem to be lying everywhere include one with an inscription naming Pontius Pilate, though this particular one is a facsimile. Most impressive of all is the huge Roman theatre which has been restored and is used for concerts and theatrical performances. It has remarkable acoustics and, with the backdrop of the Mediterranean Sea, attending a concert here is a memorable experience. There are a number of restaurants and shops within the site and the adjacent area has been developed as a tourist resort.

The main road by-passes the seaside resorts of Netanya, which is also a centre of the diamond trade, and Herzliya, before entering **Tel Aviv**. This is very much a city of the 20th century, indeed it did not exist before 1909. Now it is a modern, bustling city, with palm-lined avenues and elegant buildings, and a beach and promenade backed by hotels. The largest city in Israel it is the major commercial, economic and social centre of the country, though the seat of government remains in Jerusalem. The main shopping centre and entertainments are on and around Dizengoff Street and the 'Circle', which could be taken for any western capital city. Those pilgrims who end their tours here find it an amazing contrast to the rest of the country, though it can be a most useful overnight stop if you are having an early check-in and flight out of the country next morning. Since October 2004 there has been a splendid new terminal at Tel Aviv's Ben Gurion Airport as the main international gateway to and from the country.

The historic part of Tel Aviv is to be found at **Jaffa**, once the largest port and town, but now a mere suburb. Also called Joppa, or Yaffo, it considers itself to be the world's oldest port, the place from which Jonah set out for Tarshish; where Andromeda was held captive by Poseidon; where the Cedars of Lebanon were brought to build the Temple of Solomon. It has associations with St. Peter, for at the house of Simon the Tanner he saw the vision which led him to preach to the Gentiles (Acts 10) and where he raised the woman Tabitha. From here also Peter was summoned to Caesarea to receive the conversion of the Gentile, Cornelius. Today Jaffa has become a centre for artists and craftspeople and boasts some of the country's finest restaurants, making it a much sought after dining area. The many antiquities include remains of synagogues, churches and mosques.

Part 6
FOR FURTHER INFORMATION - ISRAEL

THE MODERN STATE

The State of Israel came into being on May 14th 1948, as a result of the Declaration of Independence. It is a Parliamentary democracy with a single chamber House – the Knesset, which has 120 members. Elections are held by a form of proportional representation under a party list system which has failed to produce a majority government in the vast majority of elections held.

The population of Israel has been growing steadily as a result of continuous immigration of Jews arriving from many parts of the world and it currently stands at around 7.5 million, including the best part of a million Arabs who are part of the permanent population and have Israeli citizenship. Some 200,000 of these are residents of East Jerusalem. This figure does not of course include the 1.5 million Arabs living in the West Bank or Gaza, areas which are now part of the Palestinian state.

BORDER CROSSINGS

There are three border crossing points between Israel and Jordan which are open to tourists. The original Allenby Bridge crossing (known in Jordan as the King Hussein Bridge) crosses the river Jordan near Jericho. Two newer crossings have been opened following the peace accord between the two countries, a northern one near Beit She'an (confusingly called the Sheik Hussein Bridge by the Jordanians) and a southern one at Arava, near to Eilat on the Red Sea. Opening hours are quite restrictive especially on Fridays and Saturdays, and often close on Jewish holidays. There are taxes and fees to be paid, and those travelling independently will need to check current regulations, either at a Tourist Office or Consulate.

There are also crossing points between Israel and Egypt, but again local conditions change often and you will need to check the current position.

CURRENCY

The Israeli currency is the shekel, called the new shekel (ILS) and this is divided into 100 agorot. Do check that you receive bank notes in the new denomination as there are still occasional shady dealers and street traders who seem to be offering high exchange rates – but they will often try to give you old notes, which are worthless.

While it is possible to obtain shekels before you leave the UK, you may find it preferable to buy most of your currency in Israel, where you will receive a better rate of exchange. There are plenty of opportunities within the country, starting with cash machines at the airport on arrival. Hotels and banks will change money readily at official rates and there are exchange offices within the Old City of Jerusalem which are also quite reliable. ATM cash machines are also readily seen in most town centres, but they may be in short supply in more rural areas. Travellers cheques and credit cards will also be accepted in most places, though not in the bazaars. Sterling and dollar notes are also acceptable in many places, though you will not get very favourable rates.

CLIMATE AND CLOTHING

Spring and autumn are the most pleasant and popular times to visit, when there is virtually no rain and temperatures are moderate. Rain is rare outside the months from December to February, but there is a wide variation in temperature from the the heights of Jerusalem – where it can be quite chilly in winter (it has even been known to snow) – and areas such as Galilee and the Dead Sea which are below sea level. Summer temperatures there can often exceed 100 degrees F (there can be quite high humidity June–August).

Clothing everywhere will be informal – men's jackets and ties are usually only worn on formal occasions, but religious sensitivity requires that at some sites men should not wear shorts and women should cover their shoulders and heads. In some cases short skirts, slacks and shorts may also be frowned upon. The most important items to take are comfortable walking shoes or sandals, sun hat and sun glasses. Otherwise, light summer clothing with a light cardigan and mackintosh if you are there in winter.

CONSULATES AND EMBASSIES

In London the Israeli Embassy is at 2, Palace Green, W8 4QB Tel ; 020-7957-9500 and in Washington at 3514, International Drive NW, DC 20008 Tel : (202) 364-5500

In Israel the British Embassy is at 192, Hayarkon St Tel Aviv 63405 Tel: (0)3 725 1222, with a Consulate at 1, Ben Yehuda St, Migador Building, 6th Floor, Tel Aviv 63801 Tel: (0)3 510 1167. Further details from the website – www.ukinisrael.fco.gov.uk

There is also a British Consulate in East Jerusalem at 19, Nashashibi Street, Sheikh Jarrah Quarter, Jerusalem 19610 Tel: (2) 541 4100 and one in Eilat. The website is at www.britishconsulate.org

For American citizens, the Embassy can be contacted on their website – www.usembassy-israel.org.il. In Jersualem the Consulate mailing address is PO Box 290 Jerusaelm 91002, but personal contact can be made at the US Consulate General office at 18, Agron Road, Jerusalem 94190 Tel: +972 2 622 7230 (972 and 2 are not needed if calling from Jerusalem).

For Canada see www.canadainternational.gc.ca/israel and Australia www.israel.embassy.gov.au and South Africa www.safis.co.il

New Zealand's Consulate in Tel Aviv is at 3 Daniel Frish St 64731 Tel. +972 3 695 6622

COMMUNICATIONS
Israeli postal and telephone services are well up to western standards. Letters and postcards will take about the same time as from Europe. Post boxes are blue with the insignia of a leaping deer, which is also found on shops and other agencies which sell stamps. Post office hours are generally from 0730 to 1900 hours, but closed on Friday afternoons and all day Saturday. The phone system is connected to the international direct dial system and you can dial from hotels – which, however, will usually make a not inconsiderable charge. If you want help from an overseas operator, call 188. Mobile networks are also available, but it is advisable to check with your mobile supplier.

ELECTRICITY
The current is 220 volts AC 50 cycles as in the UK, but in most cases you will need to have a two-pin continental adaptor with you.

EMERGENCIES
The Police emergency number is 100 or 539111. For Ambulance dial 101, Fire Service 102.

FOOD AND DRINK
In the vast majority of Jewish hotels you will be served Kosher food. This means that it has been prepared according to Jewish dietary laws – as set out in Leviticus, Chapter 11 – which in turn means that it will be hygienic and wholesome. Meat and dairy products are never served together at the same meal and have to be prepared in separate kitchens. Pork products and shellfish are regarded as "unclean" and will never be found. That apart you will find meals to be very similar to those at home, but you will not get cream in your coffee or with your dessert at dinner time, and bacon with your eggs at breakfast is definitely out! In fact, the Israeli breakfast is famous the world over

and the healthiest you can find. A buffet of eggs, fresh fruit, pickled fish, salads and vegetables and many kinds of bread and yoghurt. The orange juice is fresh – you can sometimes even squeeze it for yourself – but the coffee is often disappointing. For a quick lunch, try felafel – spiced balls of chick pea, deep fried with chopped vegetables or peppers. Or there is hummus, a chick pea puree mixed with sesame oil. Both are eaten with the flat, unleavened pitta bread.

You will not find it easy to get a good cup of coffee – it's best to ask for American coffee in the smarter hotels. In Arab areas you will be offered the very sweet Turkish coffee in a tiny cup, unless you ask for Nes, which is what it sounds like – instant, but you must ask if you want it with milk. Modern versions, like cappuccino, are gradually appearing in the western areas, but avoid something called botz, served in some cheaper snack bars. The word means mud, and that is an accurate description of the product.

Local beers, notably Maccabee or Gold Star, are very good variations of lager. Soft drinks, including the well known international brands, are everywhere, and fresh fruit juice can be found from stalls where you can see the fruit being cut and squeezed. It doesn't come any fresher or better.

Israel also has an excellent reputation for its wines, which are now exported. The Carmel range includes most of the well known grape varieties in red, white and rosé, and they are not expensive. Prices for wines and other drinks in hotels and restaurants are government controlled. In Moslem areas, remember that drink is forbidden to believers, though you will be able to obtain it in hotels. They will often serve you wines produced at the Monastery of Latrun. Some Arabs drink arak, the aniseed flavoured liquid which turns milky when mixed with water. You might like to try Sabra, the Israeli liqueur, which has a chocolate orange flavour – it is very good.

LANGUAGE
Both Hebrew and Arabic are official languages in Israel, though English is commonly spoken. You will often find street names and other notices posted in all three languages and you will rarely need to deal with anyone who does not speak English. Remember though, especially when using maps, that places often have different names in Hebrew and Arabic, though in most cases the difference is only of one or two letters.

MEDICAL CARE
Medical standards in Israel are among the highest, but costs are high and you should ensure you have adequate medical insurance cover. Take the policy with you as hospitals and doctors will often demand evidence that they will get paid. Keep receipts for all treatments. By far the greatest risk to health is the sun, so always use lotion and creams. Dehydration is another problem so keep a bottle of water with you. Insects are not an abnormal risk but it is wise to take

repellents and remedies. Water is generally safe, but it is wise not to drink it in quantity as the chemical content is different from what you are used to and may upset you. If you buy fruit in the markets be sure to wash or peel it.

NEWSPAPERS AND MAGAZINES
The English language paper is the *Jerusalem Post*, which appears daily except Saturday. The *International Herald Tribune*, like other international papers, arrives the day after publication, but is sold on news stands everywhere as are most of the normal international magazines.

PASSPORTS AND VISAS
There are no visa requirements for British, Irish or American citizens but your passport will need to have six months remaining validity on arrival. You may be asked to complete an immigration card on arrival, which will be stamped and you should then keep it with your passport, as it may be asked for when changing money. It will be collected on departure. Those who wish to use the same passport for a later visit to an Arab country should ask the immigration officer not to stamp it, as some Arab countries will not admit people with an Israeli stamp in their passports. Citizens of other countries should enquire from an Israeli embassy or tourist office as to the visa requirements for them.

PUBLIC HOLIDAYS
There being three Sabbath Days, it is advisable to plan one's itinerary with some care so as to avoid being in the wrong place on the wrong day. The Jewish Sabbath (Shabbat) runs from sundown on Friday to sunset on Saturday, and during that time all offices, most shops and much of public transport is shut down. Even hotel lifts may not be working on Shabbat, and in the Orthodox areas the driving of cars is fobidden. Any kind of noise and anything resembling work will be banned. You may find some hotel services are closed or restricted – e.g., no fresh bread for breakfast.

The Moslem holy day starts on Thursday at sunset and lasts until sunset on Friday. This is not so strictly observed, especially in the tourist areas, but many of the shops in the Old City will be closed, and it is wise not to visit the Temple Area whilst Friday prayers are in progress. Sunday is, of course, observed by Christians with the usual church services, but for the majority of residents it is a normal working day.

Jewish Holidays See the separate section which follows.

PRICES
We have avoided quoting prices in this book as they, together with exchange rates, will vary widely, though the shekel is now a reasonably stable currency. Prices generally are comparable with those in western Europe, and shops in the

tourist areas are happy to accept almost any kind of currency you like to offer, but their exchange rates will not be as good as those in the banks.

SHOPPING

This is one of the great delights of a visit to the Holy Land and most people will want to try the oriental style bazaars of the Old City for leather goods, carved olive wood, mother of pearl, ceramics, brass-ware and inlaid wood. There is a huge variation in quality as well as price, and you need to shop around if you have something particular in mind. In the bazaars you will be expected to bargain, and if you end up paying half of what you are first asked for, you will have a reasonable price. If you manage to beat the price down to a third or less, congratulate yourself on a bargain! Gold and silver jewellery with precious or semi-precious stones is on sale everywhere, but the western standard hall-marking does not apply. Most silver is what is known as Jerusalem silver, which is akin to sterling silver in content. In the larger souvenir shops such as those in Bethlehem, to which most groups are taken, prices are fixed and will be fair. The olive wood carving, much of which, like the mother of pearl jewellery, is made in Bethlehem, is of variable quality and mostly machine made. Good quality, hand made articles are not cheap, but they still represent good value.

In the Jewish centres, you will find a similar range of goods, though mostly in the higher quality ranges, together with a wide variety of modern designs in textiles, ceramics and precious metals. Israel has become one of the major world centres for diamond cutting and you will find plenty of opportunities to view and buy the end product. The standard of design in Israel is very high. Shopping hours are generally from 8am to 1pm and 4pm to 7pm or later. Shops will generally close from mid-day on Friday until Saturday evening.

TIPPING

This is unfortunately a way of life and is expected by almost everyone who provides any kind of service, though restaurant bills, taxis and theatres all include it in their prices. Most tour operators now advise their clients as to the amount they should contribute and group leaders will usually arrange for a collection to cover tips to hotel staff, guides and coach drivers, which saves a great deal of hassle. Otherwise hotel porters, waiters, the chamber maid and even the doorman who calls a taxi for you will expect a tip.

TOURIST INFORMATION

The Israel Government Tourist Office maintains a range of excellent tourist offices, both within the country and throughout the world. It also produces a huge range of literature on every area and aspect of Israeli life. A full list of offices can be found online at www.goisrael.com but the following addresses may be helpful:

London – 180 Oxford Street, W1D 1NN Tel: 020 7299 1111 www.thinkisrael.com
New York – 800 Second Ave, NY 10017 Tel: 1-212-499-5650
Los Angeles – 6380 Wilshire Blvd, Suite 1718 Tel: 1-323-658-7463
Toronto – 180, Bloor Street West, Suite 700, ON M5S 2VC Tel: 1-415-964-3784
In Jerusalem there is a Tourist Office just inside the Jaffa Gate in the Old City
and another at 17, Jaffa Road.

TRANSPORT

Israel has an excellent and comprehensive network of buses operated by the
Egged co-operative www.egged.co.il with quite low fares which will enable
access to virtually any part of the country. But as destination boards will be in
Hebrew or Arabic, you will need to ask for directions. Tickets for longer journeys
need to be purchased from the kiosks at main bus stations. The modern
Jerusalem (Central) Bus Station replaces the old one on the same site. A Light
Rail system is scheduled to open in 2011 with Line 1 running between Mount
Herzl and Air Force Street with a stop outside the Bus Station. Between the
major towns, and airports, a system of shared taxis, called Sheruts, operates,
and these are an economical and fast way to travel. Taxis are controlled and
must have meters, but drivers will always try their luck on tourists so negotiate
the fare before you get in. Rail services are still few and far between, however
new services are starting to appear, including a high-speed link planned for
2015, allowing travel from Tel Aviv and Ben Gurion Airport Terminal 3 to
Jerusalem with an underground terminus next to the Bus Station. Until then
the current Jerusalem train station is at Malha. Dial 6733794 for information.

Air travellers will arrive at Ben Gurion International Airport, Tel Aviv, which is
about 12 miles outside the city, and 37 miles from Jerusalem, to which it is
connected by a fast motorway. The airport has every facility you would expect
from a major international one, with a new terminal (3) recently completed.
Some international services can now fly direct to Eilat, which has two airports, one
international, the other almost in the town. So also does Tel Aviv, whose second
airport, Sde Dov is by the sea shore and caters for internal flights to several
destinations. Passengers must expect tight security on all flights, with stringent
baggage checks. For this reason a long check-in time is required and it is advisable
to keep a list of all purchases you have bought and to keep films separate from
cameras where possible. You will be asked to declare if you are carrying any item
for anyone else and to retain your luggage under your own supervision at all times.

JEWISH FESTIVALS AND HOLIDAYS

The dates of Festivals and Holidays in Israel are fixed according to the Jewish
calendar, which is a lunar one. A table of dates over the next few years is
appended. Note that shops, Banks and offices are closed, and public transport
may not operate, on most of these days.

ROSH HASHANA The Jewish New Year, commemorates the beginning of God's work of Creation, and is followed by ten days of repentance, leading to –

YOM KIPPUR The Day of Atonement, most solemn day of the year, and spent mostly in prayer and fasting.

HANUKA The Feast of Dedication is, on the other hand, a great celebration. It commemorates the victory of the Maccabees over the Syrians, and the re-dedication of the Temple. It is marked by the lighting of candles on the menorah, a nine-branched candlestick.

SUKKOTH Also called the feast of the Tabernacles, celebrates the protection of God during the 40 years the Jews spent in the wilderness after leaving Egypt. The people build booths – tabernacles – hung with fruit, as a reminder of how their forefathers lived in the desert before they entered Canaan.

PURIM remembers the deliverance of the Jews from extermination by the Persians, whose king cast lots to decide on the day his plan should be carried out. He was dissuaded by his Jewish Queen, Esther, whose Book is read on this day.

PESACH or **PASSOVER** lasts for seven days, the first and last being treated as public holidays. It is a celebration of the Exodus from Egypt, and thus of freedom. The special meal, called Seder, is eaten, in which all the dishes have special meaning. It was of course this meal which Jesus took with the Disciples at the Last Supper.

SHAVUOT The feast of Weeks is a kind of harvest festival, which comes seven weeks after Passover, but is also the anniversary of the giving of the Ten Commandments to Moses on Mount Sinai.

The major secular holiday in Israel is **Independence Day**, which marks the Declaration of the State of Israel in 1948.

Jewish Holidays to 2017 – with Easter and Ramadan dates								
Festival	2010	2011	2012	2013	2014	2015	2016	2017
Rosh Hashanah	09 Sept	29 Sept	17 Sept	05 Sept	25 Sept	14 Sept	03 Oct	21 Sept
Yom Kippur	18 Sept	08 Oct	26 Sept	14 Sept	04 Oct	23 Sept	12 Oct	30 Sept
Sukkot	23 Sept	13 Oct	01 Oct	19 Sept	09 Oct	28 Sept	17 Oct	05 Oct
Hannuka	02 Dec	21 Dec	09 Dec	28 Nov	17 Dec	07 Dec	25 Dec	13 Dec
Passover	30 Mar	19 Apr	07 Apr	26 Mar	15 Apr	04 Apr	23 Apr	11 Apr
Independence Day (Yom HaAtzma'ut)	11 Apr	09 May	26 Apr	15 Apr	05 May	23 Apr	12 May	01 May
Easter Day	04 Apr	24 Apr	08 Apr	31 Mar	20 Apr	05 Apr	Mar 27	16 Apr
Islamic Holidays								
Ramadan	Aug 11– Sept 08	Aug 01– Aug 29	Jul 20– Aug 18	Jul 09– Aug 08	Islamic holidays cannot be firmly determined far in advance due to the nature of the Islamic lunar calendar. Those shown here are estimated dates.			
Eid Al-Fitr marks the end of Ramadan; Eid Al-Adha marks the end of the Hajj pilgrimage								

Part 7
JORDAN

THE BACKGROUND

Since most Christian visitors will spend only a few days in Jordan, this section of the book will be rather less detailed and deal only with those places normally on their itineraries. Jordan's interest is mainly, but not entirely, in its Old Testament associations, yet it has much to offer and is a greatly under-rated tourist destination in its own right. Even though most people will have heard of Petra, few will get to the oasis of Azraq or explore the desert beyond Wadi Rum. Hopefully, what is described here will encourage readers to spend more time in the country, or return again on a longer visit.

OF PEOPLE, POLITICS AND ECONOMICS

The modern Kingdom of Jordan is in many ways a recent development. With the break-up of the Ottoman Empire at the end of the First World War, the area then became part of the British Mandate of Palestine and was known as Transjordan. After World War II the British gave semi-autonomous control of the region to King Abdullah I and in 1946 it became independent. Subsequently in 1950, Transjordan and the West Bank combined to form the independent Hashemite Kingdom of Jordan. However, as a result of the Arab-Israeli war of 1967, the country, by straddling both banks of the river Jordan, lost ten per cent of its territory and about the same proportion of its people to the Israeli occupation. That lost area included some of its most fertile and productive land, especially that around Jericho, and the major Biblical sites of Jerusalem, Bethlehem, Jericho and Samaria, though these latter three are now part of the Palestinian Authority. The loss of its two major sources of income, agriculture and tourism, dealt a severe blow to the economy of the country and at the same time it had to assimilate some 400,000 Palestinian refugees. This was the second major influx in two decades, for the population of Jordan doubled almost overnight following the Israeli Declaration of Independence in 1948, and the subsequent war between Arabs and Israelis. Additionally, more people arrived during the Gulf War of 1991 having been expelled from Kuwait and yet more still from Iraq as a result of the Second Gulf War.

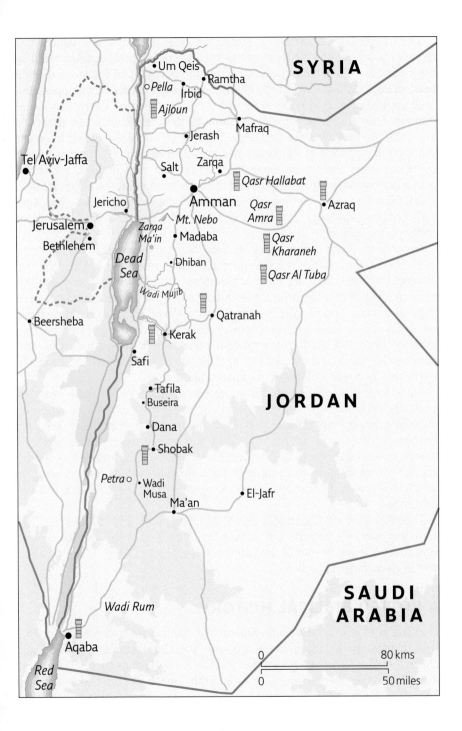

SYRIA

• Um Qeis
○ Pella   • Ramtha
        Irbid
Ajloun

• Jerash   • Mafraq

Salt   • Zarqa
Tel Aviv-Jaffa

• Jericho   Amman   Qasr Hallabat
Jerusalem   Mt. Nebo   Qasr Amra   • Azraq
Bethlehem   Zarqa Ma'in   • Madaba   Qasr Kharaneh
Dead Sea   • Dhiban   Qasr Al Tuba
Wadi Mujib
• Beersheba   • Qatranah
• Kerak

Safi

• Tafila   JORDAN
• Buseira

• Dana

• Shobak

Petra ○   • Wadi Musa
Ma'an   • El-Jafr

SAUDI ARABIA

Wadi Rum

• Aqaba

Red Sea

0   80 kms
0   50 miles

The indigenous population of Jordan are Bedouin Arabs, and whilst they remain the predominant ruling society, they are now heavily outnumbered by the incomers. As a general rule you can tell the Bedouins by the red and white head-dress, or kufiyah, whilst the Palestinians wear a black and white one. The total population is now about 5.86 million, of whom some 2.6 million live in Amman. They are overwhelmingly of Sunni Moslem religion, though about 6% are Christian, mostly Greek Orthodox. There is some evidence that in recent years the percentage of Christians has begun to decline due to the current political climate and Islamic opposition. Jordan is a constitutional monarchy with a representative government and the reigning monarch is Head of State, Chief Executive, and Commander-in-Chief of the armed forces. The King exercises his authority through the Prime Minister and the Council of Ministers, or Cabinet.

Up until his death in 1999, King Hussein long walked a precarious tightrope in Middle Eastern politics, for which he was much respected in the West. He managed to quell the more militant elements of the Palestinian cause in the early 1970s, but then became active in promoting the peace accord between them and Israel, and in 1994 the Israel-Jordan Peace Treaty came into effect. He also presided over what can only be described as something of an economic miracle which has produced a modern state with a strong industrial and commercial base, and flourishing agricultural production which generally works well as a result of desert irrigation schemes.

Since King Hussein's death, his successor, Abdullah II, has done much to continue the work of his father, both in improving the economic situation by increasing foreign investment, and in working hard to further the Middle East Process. To this end he has had several summits with US, Israeli and Palestinian delegations to find a solution for the ongoing Israeli–Palestinian conflict. In addition he has met with Pope Benedict XVI to discuss ways in which Moslems and Christians can work together for peace, tolerance and co-existence.

Today's visitor will find modern, well-equipped hotels and facilities on a par with any western capital, but it has been done without destroying the essentially oriental flavour of the country. It is a country which is well worth a visit in its own right.

A POTTED BIBLICAL HISTORY

That the land is of considerable Biblical significance there can be no doubt, though most of its associations are with the Old Testament, linked with characters like Abraham, Moses, Lot, Aaron, Elijah, Joshua, Jacob, David and Ruth. Then there were towns such as Succoth, Jabbok, Sodom and Gomorrah, Kadesh, Gilead and Midian. However, it is not entirely without its New

Testament connections as both John the Baptist and Jesus seem to have spent time east of the River Jordan and, indeed, the writer of the Fourth Gospel places Jesus' baptism on the eastern side at Bethany beyond the Jordan, and it is possible that the death of John the Baptist was here at Machaerus. Even without its West Bank territory, Jordan still claims to be part of the Holy Land and with some justification. For this is the land of the Moabites, the Edomites and the Ammorites. They all settled east of the Jordan around the 13th century BC, at about the same time the Philistines (from whom the word Palestine derives) were conquering the western side of the river. The Philistines originally came from the Aegean and were a sea-faring people who only gradually penetrated inland from the coast.

The most northerly part of the country was the Biblical land of Gilead, bounded by the river Jabbok, now called Zerga, which was crossed by Jacob on his way to reconciliation with his brother Esau (Gen. 32;33). Visitors will cross the river on the way from Amman to Jerash. Its southern boundary is Wadi Zerqa, which marks the beginning of the Ammonite Kingdom. Their capital was on the site of the present day Amman and their territory was terminated by a deep ravine, the spectacular Wadi Mujib. South of them were the Moabites, whose centre was Kerak. The southernmost kingdom, stretching from Wadi Husa at the foot of the Dead Sea, to the Gulf of Aqaba and the Red Sea, was that of the Edomites. These were the descendants of Esau (Gen. 36:9), whilst both the Moabites and Ammonites descended from Lot (Gen. 19:37-38). There were also the Amorites who lived on the western side of the Jordan, and who defeated the Moabites (Num. 21:26). On their return from exile in Egypt, the Israelites, under the leadership of Moses, tried to enter the kingdom of Edom, but were repulsed and went instead towards the kingdom of Moab, which Moses conquered, having first disposed of the Amorites. It was after the death of Moses that Joshua, with the twelve tribes, crossed the Jordan and entered Jericho.

The constant state of war between the Israelites and the Philistines continued from the death of Joshua through to the slaying of Saul and the capture by the Philistines of the Ark of the Covenant, the lowest point of the Israelites fortunes. The emergence of a new leader, David, revived them around 1000 BC when he led a golden era of conquest, capturing all three east bank states and spreading his empire to parts of Syria and as far as the Euphrates. His reign was followed by that of Solomon from 961 BC, but the glory years were ended by war between Judah in the south and the Israelites in the north. Inevitably, this part of Jordanian history was inextricably linked with that of Israel. This was the time of prophets such as Elijah and Elisha, along with pagan influences of such as Jezebel. The whole area was finally captured by the Assyrians, which brought about the virtual extinction of the Israelites as a political and military force.

It was at this time, around the 6th century BC, that we find the first references to the Nabateans, who created Petra, and who became a powerful force in the south of Jordan, commanding the vital trade routes. Judah was to fall to Nebuchadnezzar (II Kings 24:1-4) and Jerusalem was captured, Solomon's Temple destroyed, and the Jews of Judea forced into exile as slaves in Babylon, thus fulfilling the gloomy prophecies of Jeremiah. But when the Babylonians were defeated by the Persians in 539 BC, the Jews were able to return to Jerusalem and build a new Temple, usually known as the Second Temple period. There followed the campaigns of Alexander the Great, though his armies stuck mainly to the coastal route to Egypt, and finally the Romans, who took Damascus in 64 BC and Jerusalem the following year. They established, at Amman, their city of Philadelphia, which became a member of the Decapolis.

As we can see, the River Jordan, the Great Rift Valley in which it lies, along with the Dead Sea down to the Red Sea and Egypt, and the trade routes from India, have been the definitive marking posts for the historical development of the whole of this part of the Middle East. It was not until the second and third centuries AD that Christianity came to the area. It flourished under the influence of the Emperor Constantine in the fourth century and later under the Byzantines. The coming of Islam, however, following the death of Mohammed in 632, crushed the spreading of the Gospel and although the Crusaders held temporary sway, it has been the influence of Islam which has been predominant to this day.

BEGINNING IN AMMAN

Amman calls itself 'The Modern Capital, thousands of years old' and with some justification. Known in history as Rabbath-Ammon, it was the Capital of the Ammonite Kingdom from around 1200 BC. It was subsequently taken by David, though not in person, for he sent his armies to do the dirty work whilst he stayed in Jerusalem to procure for himself the beautiful Bathsheba, wife of the Hittite general, Uriah, whom he had sent to a certain death (see 2 Sam. 11:1 and 12:26 among others). Other conquerors were the Assyrians, Persians and Greeks, when Ptolemy Philadelphus, the Hellenic ruler of Egypt, named it Philadelphia after himself. Then in 106 AD, after the city had been part of the Nabatean Kingdom, it came under Roman control through the Roman General Pompey, who made it part of the Decapolis League – a loose alliance of ten free city-states bound by powerful commercial, political and cultural interests under overall allegiance to Rome. It was rebuilt in grand Roman style with colonnaded streets, baths, amphitheatre and impressive public buildings. Later still during the Byzantine period it became the seat of a

Christian bishopric and several churches were built, with the remains of one such to be found on the Citadel.

It was little more than a village when King Abdullah I selected it as the site for his new Capital in the 1920s and it very rapidly changed from being a quiet, sleepy village to a large, bustling metropolis. Its position on the main caravan routes from east to west, and between Damascus to the north and the Red Sea ports in the south, has always given it strategic importance. Amman is only 54 miles from Jerusalem and it will usually be the starting point not just for those who wish to visit Jordan alone, but also for the many Christian groups choosing an itinerary which combines Jordan with Israel in a single tour.

Amman, like Rome, is set on seven hills, the most prominent of which is called the **Citadel** and this is as good a place as any to begin a visit, since it commands a splendid view, having been the acropolis of the Roman town. The Citadel is itself an impressive archaeological site, with massive fortifications, the ruins of a second century Temple to Hercules, a huge Islamic Palace complex dating from the 8th century, with impressive carvings, as well as the remains of the Byzantine Church of St. George. Also on the summit is a small but excellent **Archaeological Museum**, which has many of the relics found on site as well as some Nabatean pottery, and so giving a picture of Jordanian life between Neolithic times and the Byzantine period.

From the top of the Citadel you can view below you down-town Amman and the other major site of the city, the **Roman Theatre**, built into the hillside in the 2nd century AD and much reconstructed. It has a seating capacity of about 6000 and is still used for outdoor concerts and spectacles. Two more museums occupy the outer wings of the Theatre and both are worth a visit. One is the **Museum of Popular Traditions** in the west wing, which has a fine display of lovely jewels, costumes and delicate embroidery from various parts of the Holy Land. On the opposite side, the east wing, is the **Folklore Museum**, displaying a collection of items which illustrate the traditional life of the local people – costumes, home furnishings, musical instruments and handicrafts dating back to the 19th century.

Outside the Theatre is a colonnaded Roman street, part of what used to be the Forum. There is not much else to see in Amman which is of Biblical or historical interest, and the geography of the place is so spread out that it does not easily encourage exploration on foot. While you are in the region of the Theatre you can visit the area called Jebel al Qal'a, where there are many souks and bazaars. One part is known as the Gold Souk, for practically every shop sells gold. The hotel area is further out and en route from your hotel to visit the sites you will certainly notice the very large, modern **King Abdullah Mosque** with its distinctive blue dome, built by King Hussein in memory of his grandfather, Abdullah I.

THE CITIES OF THE DECAPOLIS

Though under the authority of Rome, these cities still enjoyed a great deal of autonomy. As well as forming a trading league they also formed a defensive string along the south-eastern boundary of the Roman Empire, particularly against the incursions of the Nabateans, whose territory was given by Mark Antony to Cleopatra, but who soon became tired of paying the required tributes. A number of these cities are today impressive archaeological sites in a splendid state of preservation and enable us to see a picture of both Graeco-Roman life and what a Roman provincial city looked like. We have already visited Beit She'an, the only one of the Decapolis cities within Israel, but within easy distance of Amman are several others. Jerash (Gerasa of antiquity), the most impressive of all, will be given a separate section.

AJLUN is not one of them, but for all that it ought to feature as a visit on any tour north from Amman which also takes in Umm Queis and Pella. It lies some 14 miles north-west of Jerash and is an impressive and rare example of an Arab fortress, built in the 12th century by one of Saladin's generals as a defence against the Crusaders. It sits on a mountain top with spectacular views of the Jordan valley some 4000 ft below. Originally having four corner towers and a substantial moat, it protected the communication routes between south Jordan and Syria. It was later destroyed by the Mongols but rebuilt by the Mamelukes, who strengthened its fortifications. Today it provides a fascinating warren of towers, chambers, galleries and staircases for exploration, though to make the most of it the visitor needs to be reasonably fit!

UMM QUEIS is the Biblical Gadara, with its wonderfully impressive location 1700 ft above the Sea of Galilee and overlooking the Golan Heights. It was the capital of the Roman district of the Gadarenes and one possible site for the incident of the Gadarene swine (Matt. 8:28). In its time it was renowned as a cultural centre, its cosmopolitan atmosphere attracting writers, artists, philosophers and poets, one of whom described the city as 'a new Athens'. Reaching the peak of its prosperity in the 2nd century it remained a great and important city during the later Byzantine period, and was long the seat of a Bishop who attended the significant Councils of Nicea, Chalcedon and Ephesus. There is much worth seeing at Umm Qeis today, including two theatres, a paved street with double colonnade, a temple, a basilica and many other buildings which tell of a once splendid city.

PELLA is the other Decapolis city of major interest. It is a huge site, reflecting its importance in Roman times. A favourite place with archaeologists, it is exceptionally rich in antiquities, some of which are extremely old. As well as excavated ruins from the Graeco-Roman period, including a theatre, Pella provides the visitor with remains from the 4th millennium BC, along with remains of Bronze and Iron Age walled cities, Byzantine churches and houses, an early Islamic residential quarter and a small medieval Islamic mosque. It is also important to us because it, too, became an important centre of early Christianity, after the first refugees fled here from Jerusalem in the persecutions of the second century. It had its own Bishop, remaining a Christian centre throughout the Byzantine period until the Arab conquest of 635 AD. Other cities of the Decapolis included Philadelphia (modern Amman), Arbila (now Irbid), Hippos (Fiq), Bosra in Syria, and Damascus.

JERASH

One of the pleasures of a visit to Jordan, and especially of a repeat visit, is that there is so much which still lies buried and awaits discovery. Even those who have but a passing interest in archaeology cannot but be impressed by the manner in which the ancient world is clearly emerging from the ground, and Jerash is no exception to this.

Second only to Petra in tourist appeal, this ancient city set in the hills of Gilead displays remains from Neolithic, Greek, Roman, Byzantine and Omayyad times, to name just some. It first began to prosper in the days of Alexander the Great in the 3rd century BC, but it was in Roman times that it experienced its golden age. In 106 AD the Emperor Trajan annexed the wealthy Nabatean Kingdom and formed the Province of Arabia, so bringing even greater trading riches pouring into the city, and its prosperity continued to grow, reaching its peak at the beginning of the 3rd century AD. Today it is acknowledged as one of the best preserved Roman provincial cities in the world, rivalling Rome itself and on a par with the magnificent Ephesus. Given the history of the other cities just mentioned it is not surprising that Jerash became a very important centre of Christianity during the Byzantine era, and was probably at its most influential in the 3rd and 4th centuries. There remain traces of several churches, with one, named the Cathedral, dating back to 350 AD. Though the city experienced a period of decline later in the 3rd century there was something of a renaissance in the 6th during the reign of Justinian, but the Persian invasion of 614 AD ushered in the decline and an earthquake in 746 destroyed a great deal.

The city is about 30 miles north of Amman, travelling through pleasant countryside and crossing the Jabbok River, as was described earlier. Excavations began in the 1920s, though the site had been previously discovered by a German explorer early in the 19th century. Its paved and colonnaded streets, temples, theatres, spacious public squares and plazas, baths and fountains, city walls and gates remain in exceptional condition. Though Jerash is a very large site and will take at least three hours to do it any kind of justice, the walking is fairly easy. A full day would not be wasted and there are adequate facilities available for refreshment.

Jerash – The Forum

The first thing you will come to is **Hadrian's Arch**, which is, in fact, a triple archway built to commemorate the visit of the Emperor Hadrian in AD 129, a visit which helped the city to flourish even more. The ancient **Hippodrome**, which could accommodate 15,000 spectators and where Gerasa held its chariot races and other sporting events, is also visible before you arrive at the main entrance to the site. Jerash has two **Theatres**: the southern one, closest to the entrance, requires a slight climb to the top, but it is well worth it for the wonderful panoramic view of the whole site. The theatre has been restored and partly reconstructed, and even seat numbers can be found on many of its 3000 places. From the top there is an excellent view of the superb oval **Plaza**, often referred to as the **Forum**, one of the outstanding features of the city. Some 260 ft wide and 290 ft long it is surrounded by 56 reconstructed Ionic columns, and is the only Roman forum so well preserved to be seen anywhere. From it leads the **Cardo**, or main street, also paved and lined with columns, this time Corinthian, and which stretches a distance of about a mile towards the northern or Damascus Gate. An aqueduct once ran along the top of the columns. It is a remarkable street, for in its stones you can see the ruts made by the the wheels of chariots; under the flagstones are the channels for drainage; on either side are the buildings – temples, baths, shops, fountains – of a busy city centre. You can almost feel that you are there among the crowds, transported in time, listening to the march of the legionnaires' feet, the clash of gladiatorial swords, and the cries of market traders selling their wares. Jerash is a remarkable experience and not one to be missed.

Between the southern Theatre and the oval Forum is the **Temple of Zeus**, which dates from the first century AD, with great vaulted corridors beneath. Walking along the Cardo, the first item of note, on your left, is the **Agora**, or market place, with a lion's head fountain at its entrance. You then come to the main intersection, the South Tetrapylon, marked by four pedestals which once supported granite towers. The road on the right leads over a bridge and out of town, whilst that to the left leads uphill to the remains of some houses. Further along the Cardo is a richly carved gateway to the Temple of Dionysus, which was rebuilt in the 4th century as the Byzantine **Cathedral**. Here is the centre of the Christian area of Jerash, as to the west is the large Church of St. Theodore, and beyond that is the complex of three churches dedicated to Saints Cosmos and Damian, St. John the Baptist and St. George. They share a common atrium and have splendid mosaic floors. Altogether some fifteen churches have been uncovered in Jerash and there may be more still buried.

Returning to the Cardo, or Street of Columns as it is commonly known, brings us to the **Nymphaeum**, an elaborately carved semi-circular fountain on which fragments of painting can still be seen. The **Temple of Artemis**, goddess of Jerash, is one of the largest and most imposing of the buildings on the site, approached by a monumental staircase with 22 towering Corinthian columns. A little further along, on the opposite side of the street, are the **Western Baths**, built in the 2nd century, and opposite is the **Northern Theatre**, smaller than its southern counterpart, seating approximately 1200 people, but impressive nonetheless.

Archaeologists of many nations continue to work on the site and more and more of Jerash comes into view with each succeeding year. A spectacular visit can be made on summer nights when *son et lumière* performances are given, some in English. These last about an hour and a half and require the audience to walk around the site from stage to stage. There is also the Jerash Festival, usually in July, with cultural performances by international artists to a background of living history.

THE DESERT CASTLES

Travelling east from Amman to the desert oasis of Azraq provides a particularly interesting excursion and enables visits to several of the so-called 'Caliph's Castles' which are set, seemingly, in the middle of nowhere. They date from the first half of the 8th century AD, but what remains provides an intriguing insight into the way of life of the ancient aristocracy. There are a number of sites, but this section concentrates on those which can more easily be seen by travelling along the excellent highway between Amman and Azraq. Built by the Umayyad dynasty of Caliphs, they were the first Arab rulers to set up their capital in Damascus, and these castles were their country estates to be used as hunting lodges, bath houses and pure pleasure palaces – though in some instances 'pure' may not be the most appropriate word! They could be resting places on a journey, motels for the traders and their caravans, or simply to escape the restrictions of life in Damascus which the strictures of Islamic law imposed. Here they could indulge themselves away from the watchful eyes of the more pious minded. Together they represent a fine collection of early Islamic art and architecture.

Qasr Mushatta is the first we come to (Qasr means castle). It is just off the main road, which incidentally in this area has been built sufficiently wide that it can be used as an aircraft runway in time of war. Mushatta is the largest and most ambitious of the castles and everywhere are signs of an architectural splendour that was never fully realised. Nowadays only small fragments of fresco remain. Much of the carved plaster was shipped to Germany as a gift to Kaiser Wilhelm and can now be seen in the Pergamum Museum in Berlin.

Qasr el-Kharana is the only one which appears to have had a defensive role, with immensely strong walls and only one entrance. The rooms are arranged around a central courtyard and stairs lead to an upper storey. It is not decorated and its situation on the major caravan route indicates that it may have been intended as a resting place for travellers rather than for pleasure purposes. A further theory is that it was a secure meeting place where Umayyad leaders could discuss state affairs.

Qasr Amra, probably the most beautiful and now a UNESCO World Heritage Site, was and still is, pure pleasure for the eye. It was clearly a bath house for it has a caldarium (hot room), a tepidarium (warm room) and a frigidarium (cold room), together with changing rooms, an audience hall and a complex water system. The whole interior, both walls and ceiling, is covered with rich frescoes, many of which have been restored in recent years. Paintings include themes such as hunting, dancing, musicians, cupids, bathing scenes and a full zodiac covers the dome of the hot room. There is a remarkable portrayal of humans, given that after the advent of Islam any illustration of living beings was prohibited. If the paintings are illustrative of the kind of life which was led here, it is just as well it was long after the time of the Old Testament prophets, or their tidings would have been dire in the extreme. There are naked dancers, buxom women with babies, and a cupid leads a young man to a girl sleeping in her bed. Well, you can guess the rest!

And so we come to **Azraq**, whose black basalt castle is now little more than a shell, yet it has been the most recently used, since it was an HQ for Lawrence of Arabia during his assault on the Turks in the First World War. Lawrence was a frequent visitor to Azraq, as he describes in the *The Seven Pillars of Wisdom*, and his quarters within the castle, just above the main entrance, are reached through a huge, heavy stone door with an ingenious stone hinge system. The castle is, of course, of much earlier origin and and later much rebuilt. What you now see was redesigned by the Mamelukes in the 13th century, but both the Romans and Nabateans had forts here and the Caliphs would have made use of them. The oasis here is the only permanent, natural wetland in Jordan, but from the 1970s onward became heavily degraded as a result of over-pumping to supply water to cities like Amman and Irbid. This has been made even worse by the developments in industry and tourism along with urban growth. Clearly this has had a detrimental effect on both wildlife and people. By 1970 the marshlands were all but dried up and by 1992 so too had the fragile wetlands. Prior to this the oasis had been a major attraction and stopping-off point for migrating birds, but who then began to by-pass Azraq for other locations. However, major conservation enterprises have been put in hand, for example, by pumping water back in so that the marshland has begun to return, so renewing the habitat for many types of wildlife, including blue-necked ostriches and water buffalo, along with thousands of migrating birds. There is still much to achieve, but at least the problem has been recognised and appropriate steps have begun to be taken.

THE KING'S HIGHWAY

While it is possible to visit Petra in a day tour from Amman, that is if you don't mind a round trip of about 360 miles, it does mean using the fast but uninteresting Desert Highway. Much more preferable is the alternative route via the sometimes winding but always scenic King's Highway, an historic road stretching from Amman to Aqaba. Though it requires a full day to reach Petra, if the proper stops are made en route, it will, however, be one of the most memorable days of your tour and a fascinating prelude to your arrival in Petra.

But before embarking on that particular journey we first of all drive south-west from Amman towards the Dead Sea and to the area of **Bethany beyond the Jordan**, which John's Gospel identifies as the place of Jesus' Baptism by John the Baptist (Jn. 1:28) and where Jesus fled for safety after being threatened with stoning in Jerusalem (Jn. 10:40). Recent archaeological surveys and excavations along the length of Wadi al-Kharrar since 1996 have led to increasing, though as yet not universal, archaeological and scholastic acceptance that this is the place of the Baptism. A gentle walk of about 1.5 miles along the wadi brings you to the bank of the River Jordan itself, and in the area have been discovered a number of shallow baptismal pools, dating from Roman and Byzantine times, and the remains of several Byzantine churches. There is also the delightful modern Greek Orthodox Church of St. John the Baptist, with Byzantine-style frescoes portraying scenes from the life of John the Baptist and Jesus.

Church of St John the Baptist, Bethany beyond the Jordan

So we continue our way south, picking up one of the oldest trading routes in the world, but also used by armies and pilgrims, the King's Highway. Its first Biblical reference is in the Book of Numbers (21:1–7) when Moses and the people of Israel request but are refused passage through Edom and therefore used the King's Highway. The Jordanian section includes some of the most spectacular scenery in the Middle East. For our first stop we turn off the route to **Mount Nebo**, about 25 miles south of Amman. From here there is a spectacular view indeed: virtually the whole of the Jordan Valley away to the north, with the Dead Sea more than 3000ft below and disappearing to the south. Also visible down in the valley is the oasis of Jericho. Almost straight ahead, on a clear day, you can make out the spires on the top of the Mount of Olives in Jerusalem, a good 30 miles away. Looking from this position across the valley is the view Moses would have seen when the God sent him to view the Promised Land, but 'you shall see the land from a distance, but you may not enter the land I am giving to the Israelites' (Deut. 32:49 & 34:1). The present church, built to honour Moses, dates back originally to the 4th century and was much enlarged by the Byzantines, with reconstruction work being carried on since 1933. Wonderful mosaics depicting animals, farmers and hunters is dated back to the 6th century. Outside the church a modern sculpture of the serpent entwined around a cross brings together both the Old and New Testaments, Moses and Jesus. This was created to commemorate the visit of Pope John Paul II in March 2000.

On a mountain top nearby was the Biblical Machaerus, where Herod had a Palace and where, it is said, Salome danced and John the Baptist was beheaded. Well, maybe – but that is said also of Sebastiya in Samaria!

We then return to the main route and this brings us to the town of **Madaba**, known the world over as 'The City of Mosaics'. It was a border town of the Moabites at the time of the return of the Israelites from Egypt, under its Biblical name of Medba (Num. 21:30, Josh. 13:9 & 16:1). It was a Roman settlement, but under the Byzantines it flourished as a major Christian settlement and it was from this time that most of its mosaics are dated. The most famous is in the present day Greek Orthodox Church of St. George. This is a 6th century map of the Holy Land from Egypt and the Nile to Palestine and Jerusalem and which, though damaged by an earthquake, is still extremely well preserved. The colouring and details are remarkable, and though incomplete the mosaic shows places such as Bethlehem, Jericho, Beersheba, the Dead Sea, Kerak, the Jordan River and in particular Jerusalem. This latter has been of immense value to scholars for it showed for the first time the location of the main street of Old Jerusalem, the Cardo, along with the city walls, various gates and the Church of the Holy Sepulchre. There is also an **Archaeological Park**, in which are several more remains of 6th century churches and mosaics.

South of Madaba the road enters its most scenic section, with deep wadis and gorges, towering cliffs and mountains. We pass through **Dhiban**, which was the Biblical Dibon (Num. 21:26–30 & 32:34), the former Moabite capital,

The Mosaic Map of the Holy Land at Madaba

where excavations have revealed layers of civilisation back to 3000 BC. A large carved stone was found here with some of the earliest Hebrew inscriptions detailing the battles between the Moabites and Israelites around 850 BC. Then we soon come to **Wadi Mujib**, known as the 'Grand Canyon of the Middle East'. It is a precipitous gorge some two miles wide and 3300 ft deep, with a river at the bottom which empties into the Dead Sea. As an obvious and easily defensible boundary between the warring kingdoms it is mentioned in the Bible as Arnon (Num. 21:3–15 & Deut. 2:24–36). Geologists will appreciate the different layers which line the steep sides of this part of the Rift Valley.

The next major stop is at the commanding Crusader fortress of **Kerak**. It had various names in the Old Testament, including Kir-Mob and Kir Haresand (2 Kings 3:25 and Isaiah 15:1), and its current name in Arabic, Krak de Moab. These all indicate its importance as one of the chief cities of the Moabites, but it was under the Crusaders that it became fortified with one of the largest and most imposing castles in the Middle East. During their time here the Crusaders held sway as far south as the Gulf of Aqaba and so controlled the trade routes from Egypt to both Damascus and Jerusalem, so these fortresses had a toll-extracting role as well as a defensive one. Castles like Kerak are an example of the Crusaders' architectural genius. Each one was built to be a day's journey from its neighbour and at night a beacon was lit to signal to Jerusalem that it was safe. Kerak finally fell to Saladin in late 1188 at the end of an eight month siege and the treacherous and brutal Reynald de Châtillon, the fortress's most infamous occupant, was beheaded by Saladin himself. The fort is a dark maze of stone-vaulted halls and passageways, and corridors which lead into one another through heavy arches and doorways. The upper level is predominantly Crusader and some of the best preserved remains are underground from the Mamelukes. From the outside there are splendid views all around.

After crossing another deep valley, Wadi Hasa, we are in the most southerly of the Biblical kingdoms, that of the Edomites. At Tafila, about 40 miles south of Kerak, is another Crusader ruin, set in one of the more fertile parts of the land, whilst at Buseira are remains which show that it was one of the most important of Edomite settlements. The castle at Shobak, another huge Crusader fortification, is now mainly ruined. It stands high above a desolate landscape and has one of the deepest wells ever dug by the Crusaders, with 375 steps leading down to the water supply.

We are now nearing Petra and there are spectacular views from the road of the lunar-like rock formations which surround the canyon in which the Rose Red city lies. Before arriving there, however, we must take a diversion to **Beida** or 'Little Petra', so-called because it appears like a smaller version of the main city about 5 miles away. Traces of settlements going back 9000 years have been found by the well-known archaeologist Diana Kirkbride, the earliest being from the Neolithic period around 7000 BC. Six different levels and several styles of building, together with stone tools and other implements, have given a unique insight into the lifestyle of that age. The gorge leading into the town is much shorter than that at Petra, but once inside the town there are façades of houses, temples and cisterns, giving the impression that this was very much a residential area. The village which lies at the entrance to Petra is called **Wadi Musa** or the 'Spring of Moses', after a tradition that this was where Moses struck the rock and brought forth water.

PETRA

'A Rose Red City, Half as Old as Time' – that most famous and apt description of Petra was written by Dean John William Burgon, one-time Dean of Chichester Cathedral, in a sonnet about this place which he had only heard described but had never himself visited. Having lain hidden from the world for several centuries Petra was re-discovered in 1812 by Johann Ludwig Burckhardt, a Swiss explorer. He was a classic 19th century adventurer, the kind of man who would spend years polishing his disguise as an Arab so he could pass unnoticed through the Middle East, a land not always hospitable to Europeans. During his travels Burckhardt had heard rumours of a lost city in the mountains and under the pretext of wanting to make a sacrifice at the Tomb of Aaron persuaded his guide to take him there. And the rest, as they say, is history – literally!

Lying deep in the mountains of southern Jordan, Petra is indeed a beautiful and awe-inspiring place. Its heyday was during the time of the Nabateans who for some 500 years developed Petra as the centre of their civilisation, possibly with a population of about 20-30,000 people. Though originally they seem to have been farmers, the Nabateans became skilled traders who brought vast wealth to the city. Because of its location Petra was a commercial crossroads and its control of this trading route meant that caravans laden with silks, spices, incense, gold, copper and ivory would rest here, a skilfully created oasis in the desert and a most remarkable city carved out of solid sandstone rock – temples, tombs, houses, baths. Creating a capital in such an inhospitable area of arid desert meant that they had to become experts at water management and so they built a complex system of channels and cisterns to supply the water they needed.

It was always likely that Rome would at some stage want to take direct control of this outpost of its Empire and in 106 AD the Emperor Trajan made Petra part of the Roman Province of Arabia, and the great theatre in the heart of the city is testimony to the Romans influence while they were here. But about a century later decline set in, though no one seems clear about the precise reasons. Christianity reached here in the 4th century and a number of churches have been discovered, though later Islam became the dominant religion. There is also evidence of later Crusader presence in the city, but soon after the end of the 14th century Petra became lost to the western world and remained so until the arrival of Burckhardt in 1812.

Entrance into the Siq is through the remains of a monumental arch which brings you into a narrow gorge about a mile long with towering cliffs on either side, some rising to almost 600 ft and in places all but touching one another across the chasm. As you walk through you begin to discover evidence of the Nabateans' past, such as the niches with carved outlines of ancient gods, as well as the vital water channels which were part of their system both for gathering water and for the prevention of floods. A memorable feature of Petra ('rock') is the different colouring of the rock strata in the changing light as the sun rises and sets. Depending on whether you are here in the morning or the late afternoon you will marvel at the changing hues of the sandstone.

The first sight of Petra, as you emerge from the narrowness and dimness of the gorge, is the sudden, wonderful sight of **Al-Khazneh**, popularly known as **The Treasury**. This is undoubtedly the city's most famous and photogenic sight. Featured in the film *Indiana Jones and the Last Crusade*, this towering façade is much more likely to have been a tomb or even more probably a temple. The Treasury, like so many of the buildings, tombs and temples which enrich the city, was carved straight out of the rock face. The Nabatean style of carving was that in the main they started from the top and worked down, and the vertical rows of square holes alongside the façades – particularly evident at the Treasury – were the means by which the craftsmen reached the top of the site. View this in the morning about 10 am and you will see it turning from pink to a yellowish colour, and in the late afternoon the rock turns to purple shades.

Taking the road to the right of the Treasury you will pass along **The Street of Façades**, with various monuments and many of the city's tombs and caves. A path to the left before you get to the Theatre leads up to the highest point of Petra, the **High Place of Sacrifice**. Everyone seems to have a different count on the number of rock-cut steps to the top, but to say that there are at least 800 allows a certain leeway! The steep climb is well worth while for the view from the top is stupendous as you view the lunar-like landscape around you. You are now about 3400 ft above sea level. There is a large altar with carvings and a channel for draining blood, presumably animal as there is no evidence of human sacrifice here. If you continue back down on the far side of the mountain, instead of returning the way you have just come, you will find the **Lion Monument**, originally a fountain, with the shape of its head and legs still to be seen. Next you reach the lovely **Garden Triclinium**, so-called because of the greenery around it, and then further along is the **Tomb of the Roman Soldier**, given this name because in one of the niches of the façade is part of the carved figure of a high-ranking Roman officer. Not to be missed either is the Triclinium, which has the only carved interior in Petra, and the walls and

Petra – The Treasury (left) and The Monastery (right)

ceiling are enriched with the most beautiful bands of colour. Continuing down from here takes you further along Wadi Farasa and then out into the main valley.

However, if you are lacking time and energy for the hike to the High Place, or indeed, if you return from the High Place the way you went up, you will come to the central area and find firstly the **Roman Theatre**. Though begun by the Nabateans to hold 3000 people, it was later enlarged by the Romans to hold up to 8500. Again, if you have the energy, a climb to the upper tiers is rewarded with fine views both of the theatre and the central area of Petra. Then comes the **Nymphaeum**, a public drinking fountain, and a Roman triumphal arch, through which you enter the **Cardo Maximus**, the paved and colonnaded Roman High Street of the city. We are now in a large open area and beneath our feet must be the remains of countless other buildings yet to be excavated. A restaurant offers some relief before tackling another climb of similar proportions to that of the High Place. This one takes us to the **Deir**, or **Monastery**, Petra's most gigantic Temple, thought to date back to the 1st century AD, and approximately 154 ft high and 158 ft wide. It is believed to be a typical example of Nabatean architecture and possibly dedicated to the deified King Obodas I. In all probability it became known as the Monastery because of the large number of crosses carved on its walls, suggesting that at some time it could have been used as a church. But as well as marvelling at this magnificent building there is the opportunity to take in the views from the top of this mountain, views which are no less stunning than those from the

High Place, with wadis some 4000 ft below draining into the Great Rift Valley, and looking beyond that to the Negev. It is an ideal point from which to reflect on the isolation of these desert lands, the reason why they have been able to keep their secrets hidden for so many centuries.

Among the many other monuments to be seen are the **Royal Tombs**, carved from the southern rock face. Because of the vastness of their size they are believed to be tombs for wealthy or important people of the city, possibly Petran royalty. One such tomb, the **Urn Tomb**, was converted into a Christian Church in 446 AD. Other tombs are the **Silk Tomb**, so described for its bands of natural brilliant colouring which give its walls the appearance of shot silk, and the **Palace Tomb**, in Roman style and Petra's largest façade, three storeys high.

Within the scope of this particular book it is impossible to mention everything you could see in Petra. But one further discovery should be mentioned and that is a Byzantine Church, maybe even a Cathedral, dating to the 5th and 6th centuries, containing some extraordinary Byzantine mosaics. Excavation work is still being carried out here. Suffice to say a day is not enough to see all that Petra has to offer, but it is all that the vast majority of visitors will have. You can make the most of your time there by proper preparation, making sure you have the basic necessities of water, head covering and comfortable shoes. The heat will be strong and some of the walking is quite rough, even without the climbs to the High Place and the Monastery, each of which will take about an hour. The only other advice is to take the visit at a slow and relaxed pace. If you don't want to walk all the way through Petra it is possible to hire a donkey or a camel, and if you do choose to walk there are a number of stopping places en route for a drink and a sit down!

It should be noted, too, that for the less able-bodied, instead of walking down through the Siq, you can hire a horse-drawn buggy which will take you down to the Treasury and return you afterwards. But however you choose to explore this truly amazing city it will undoubtedly be one of the most memorable and unforgettable days of your life.

AQABA AND WADI RUM

Petra to Aqaba is about a two hour drive, and where the road passes through Ras el Naqab, a few miles after joining it from Petra, is a particularly scenic stretch with splendid views. Now it is mainly a downhill run to **Aqaba**, the only port Jordan has, on the only small piece of coastline it can boast. From the sea front can be seen the coasts of Israel, Egypt and Saudi Arabia. A mere 4 miles away is the great Israeli resort of **Eilat**, where much of what is said about marine life and water-sports in Aqaba is also true there. Both are excellent winter get-aways.

Being the only port to serve not just Jordan but Syria, Iraq and parts of Saudi as well, Aqaba has something of an industrial feel about it, though the hotel and beach areas have been kept separate. For more than 5,500 years it has played an important part in the economy of the region and has been a principal junction for land and sea routes from Asia, Africa and Europe, a role still played today, and the export of phosphates, mined further north and brought here by rail, is an important part of its present day economy. The temperate climate and gentle water currents have created the perfect environment for the growth of corals and a plethora of marine life. Little wonder that the Gulf of Aqaba is a prime location for snorkelling, scuba diving and surfing. And if you prefer to stay on the water rather than in it, then glass-bottomed boats will enable you to experience something of the marvels that lie beneath the clear waters.

But Aqaba has a past as well as a present. The Archaeological Museum illustrates its history and there is a Mameluke Fort. T. E. Lawrence was based here for a time after wresting the port from the Ottomans during the First World War. It is also believed that there are the remains of one of the oldest Christian churches in the Holy Land, probably dating from the late 3rd or very early 4th century, though in June 2008 archaeologists profess to have discovered a cave underneath Saint Georgeous Church in Rihab, north-east of Amman, which may have been part of an even earlier church. Mind you, a church about the same age as the Aqaba one is also claimed to have been discovered behind the walls of a maximum security prison at Megiddo where, for example, a mosaic was uncovered displaying the early Christian symbols of fish.

From Aqaba there is a ferry across the Red Sea to Nuweiba in Egypt, from which it is an easy drive to **Mount Sinai** and **St. Catherine's Monastery**. A two day trip from here, with a night spent in Nuweiba or the tourist village near St. Catherine's, is eminently worthwhile and particularly so if you are prepared to be up well before dawn for the climb to the top of Mt. Sinai to experience sunrise (camels are also available!) and relive the Biblical story of Moses and the Ten Commandments (Ex. 20). But remember you will need a double entry visa for Jordan as well as Egypt. There is also a border crossing between Aqaba and Eilat which makes for much easier travelling and has brought about the possibility of tour itineraries combining Israel, Jordan and Egypt.

However, the major excursion from Aqaba, unless you make the visit en route from Petra, is to **Wadi Rum**, about an hour's drive away. This is best remembered as the film set for *Lawrence of Arabia* and indeed it is authentic, as it was the route used by T. E. Lawrence, who in his book, *The Seven Pillars of Wisdom*, described the area as 'vast, echoing and god-like', one of his many lyrical descriptions. It is undoubtedly the largest and most magnificent

Wadi Rum

of Jordan's desert landscapes, with rock formations rising like some strange, awe-inspiring moonscape 2000 ft above the floor of the valley, which is itself already about 3000 ft above sea level. One such spectacular peak is often referred to as The Seven Pillars of Wisdom, after Lawrence's book of that title. You can sample something of this incredible scenery either by camel or four-wheel drive Jeep, and many people have found that one of the most remarkable experiences of their life has been to spend a night under the stars in a Bedouin tent. But do not venture anywhere into the Desert without a guide, for the many tracks will soon get you lost. No doubt you will also meet up with members of the colourful Desert Patrol with their khaki uniforms, red bandoliers, dagger and rifle, and the red and white chequered head-dress of the Jordanian Bedouin. They are friendly and hospitable and will usually answer your questions. Clearly such a region is not without some striking archaeological finds, mainly from the Nabatean period and including the ruins of a temple. The area has one of the major concentrations of semi-nomadic Bedouin and you will probably see their tents, goats and sheep.

Whether visiting Israel alone, or Israel with Jordan, as Christian pilgrims we will find much to enrich our understanding of the background to the Gospels and the ministry of Jesus, as well as that of the Old Testament. It will assuredly be a journey of a lifetime, of that there can be no doubt, and hopefully in reflecting on the past, such an experience informs our awareness of the present and inspires us to a renewed commitment to live as the People of God, both locally and globally.

PRACTICAL INFORMATION FOR JORDAN

For most purposes the information given in relation to Israel will also apply to Jordan but where it differs, the following remarks apply:-

BORDER CROSSINGS
There are three into Israel – at Aqaba, the Allenby Bridge (King Hussein Bridge), and the northern one known as the Sheik Hussein Bridge. These are detailed on page 62.

CURRENCY
The Jordanian currency unit is the Dinar, which is divided into 1000 fils. You may sometimes come across the denomination piastre, which is 10 fils. Bank notes come in denominations from 500 fils to 50 dinars and coins from 250 fils down to five. The lower denominations are of copper, the others in a silver alloy.

EMBASSIES AND CONSULATES
London: The Hashemite Kingdom of Jordan Embassy and Consulate can be found on the website www.jordanembassy.org.uk Telephone - 0207 937 3685 Washington: The Embassy and Consulate are both at 3504 International Drive NW, Washington DC 20008. Telephone contact on (202) 966-2664 or (202) 966-2887 (visas). The website is www.jordanembassyus.org

EMERGENCIES
Fire, Police, First Aid, can all be called on 199. Ambulance is 75111. A 24-hour Emergency Police Mobile service which is English speaking is on 21111 or 37777.

FOOD AND DRINK
Most hotels serve a buffet style meal at both lunch and dinner, usually including both western and eastern style dishes, with plenty of fruit and salads. There will be several types of hummus with dips for filling a pitta bread sandwich. Felafel is also a popular mid-day snack – this is a deep fried ball of chickpeas and herbs in an unleavened bread outer. The supply of fresh fruit and vegetables is plentiful, but it should be washed or peeled, and the use of bottled water is advisable. All hotels have bars but you will have difficulty in finding one outside, though there are a few liquor shops in Amman centre. Alcoholic drinks are not easily available in this Moslem country, though some local beers can be bought, and the wines offered in hotels will probably come from Latrun on the West bank. Expect any kind of alcoholic drink to be expensive. Coffee will be small, very black, and sweet, unless you ask for American style.

LANGUAGE
The national language is of course Arabic, but English is widely spoken particularly among younger people and always by hotel staff. There is an English language daily newspaper – *The Jordan Times*.

PASSPORTS AND VISAS
British, American or European Union visitors do not need to obtain visas in advance – they are issued at the airport or port on arrival. Those of other nationality can obtain information on the website – www.jordanembassy.org.uk/forms

PUBLIC HOLIDAYS (also see page 69)
National holidays are on January 1st, May 1st, May 25th (Independence), in

addition to the Moslem religious holidays as shown on page 69. Friday is the religious holiday when most shops and offices are closed.

SHOPPING
As in Israel much of the souvenir shopping will be for locally crafted goods in olive wood, brass, textiles and glass. Prices are a little higher than in Israel but not prohibitive. Shops are generally open from 9am to 1pm and 3pm to 7pm, but closed on Fridays. Some also close on Sundays and during the month of Ramadan expect hours and services to be restricted.

TOURIST INFORMATION
The Jordan Tourist Board does not maintain public offices outside the country, but it can be contacted in Amman at P.O. Box 830688, Amman 11183. The easiest way to obtain information is via their website – www.visitjordan.com. The offices of Royal Jordanian Airlines in major capital cities will also be found helpful.

TRANSPORT
In spite of what we have said about most people speaking English, you will need help if you are proposing to use public transport. All the signs are in Arabic and few of the crews will speak English. It would be as well to get the hotel staff to write down the name of your destination and instructions as to where to board your bus. Much the easier way is to use taxis which are not expensive, though drivers tend to compete with their Italian counterparts in their haste to get you to where you want to go. As in Israel there are also shared taxi schemes between the major towns. The JETT coach company runs scheduled services between major towns and also has a daily service between Amman and Damascus. (Tel : 64146 for information).

Air Travel Amman's strikingly modern airport is the arrival point for the vast majority of international flights. It is on the south-eastern side of the city, and has all the services to be expected from a major international terminal. There is an airport tax payable on departure, as there will be on your outward journey, but as these things change without warning it is not possible to give amounts. You do need to check this in advance as you will need to keep back enough dinars to pay in cash. Check with your airline website for up to date information.

The only other airport in Jordan which visitors are likely to use is at Aqaba, from which it is possible to get connecting flights via Amman. Services between London and Amman are supplied by Royal Jordanian and British Airways, as well as some American ones. Royal Jordanian also flies to most of the major western destinations, and has a modern fleet and efficient service.

Part 8
THE FLORA AND FAUNA
OF THE HOLY LAND

The Late Margaret Smith contributed this article to the last edition of the Pilgrim's Guide to the Holy Land in 1998. We reprint it here with the agreement of the Revd Raymond Smith.

Both Israel and Jordan have a wealth of species, more than 2500 in fact, of both flora and fauna which are indigenous to the area. But what you will see will depend upon which area you are in and when you are there.

TREES AND SHRUBS

In both countries the Australian Acacia, or blue leaved wattle, is seen in the desert areas. Its wood was probably used to construct the tabernacle (Ex:25.10) and its leaves are eaten by ibex, camels and other desert animals. The wonderful scarlet blossom of the Royal Poinciana or flame tree, lights up even the urban streets in June and July, whilst the Judas Tree, with its twisted branches and from which Judas is reputed to have hanged himself can also be found- on Mount Carmel among other places. The white flowers, which appear directly from the branches, are said to represent the tears of Christ. The Carob, or Locust Tree, also thrives in the dry climate and is also cultivated for the beans, which are edible and sometimes used as a chocolate substitute. Also known as the St. John's Bread Tree (see Mt;3.4) the fruit has kept alive the horses of the Crusaders, and John the Baptist may have eaten them with honey. Another tree with Biblical connections is the Sodom Apple, which is seen around the Dead Sea and the Jordan Valley, it has large green leaves, curious flowers and inedible fruit (Deut;32.32). The Thorn Apple, which you may find on desert areas and wasteland in Jordan, is on the other hand, very poisonous. The Greek philosopher, Theophrates, wrote of it "three 2oths of an ounce, the patient becomes sportive. Double the dose and the result is madness". You have been warned !

Bougainvillea and Hibiscus are in profusion everywhere though they are not native, as are cypress and eucalyptus, and of course the olive, which can live for several hundred years, as in Gethsemane. You may see them being harvested with large sheets spread under and the trees being shaken or beaten.

The best time to see flowers is of course the spring, from early March onwards, when the citrus trees are also in flower. The powerful scent of the orange blossom when the early crop of ripe fruit is also on the trees is memorable. There will be a profusion of wild flowers in the fields and hillsides, such as the horned poppy (in both scarlet and orange forms), the crown anemone, turban buttercup and pink asphodel. The most common flower in Israel is probably the Star of Bethlehem, but one of the rarest is the Madonna Lily, which can sometimes be seen in late spring. It is said to be the flower carried by the angel at the Annunciation. The Nazareth Iris can be found in that area and throughout Galilee, but in Jordan you will be lucky if you see the national flower – the black iris. It grows in large colonies at Jerash, Madaba and Petra, but is found nowhere else in Europe.

It goes without saying that virtually all the species mentioned, and most others as well, are protected by law, so you must not pick them. Local people however, do pick species such as the giant fennel whose leaves they use in shomar salad, the common mallow, which they use for cooking "Khubaiseh" and dandelion of several varieties which are commonly used as a vegetable.

BIRDS AND ANIMALS
One of the finest sights in the Middle East is to be there at the time of the migration of the **Birds** along the Great Rift Valley in spring and autumn. Key areas are the Golan Heights, Upper Galilee and Eilat, and famously, the oases of Azraq in Jordan which is a mecca for bird lovers of all nationalities. As well as the normal European species, you can see eagles, vultures, stork, warblers and cranes. At other times and in other areas you can still find a huge variety of delightful birds, such as several types of large kingfisher. The lesser pied one has black and white plumage, and the white breasted or smyrna kingfisher is bright blue with white breast and a huge red bill. These, as well as the better known green/blue one we are used to, can usually be seen around the Sea of Galilee, as also can the black and white night herons, the black headed gulls, little egrets and the pygmy cormorant. On top of Masada, look for the Tristram's Grackle, a starling with a bright orange stripe on its underwings, first noted and named by a Canon of Durham Cathedral. You may also see hooded crows, hoopoes, shrikes and bulbuls – the yellow vented one with a black head is often both seen and heard. There is a profusion of brightly coloured tits,

finches and warblers, as well as the Palestinian Sunbird, a small hummingbird with a long beak which you may often see in the hibiscus bushes at Tabgha and elsewhere.

The **Animal World** will not be so easily apparent, though you ought to see plenty of Hyrax sunning themselves on the rocks in the hills around Galilee and almost anywhere else. It is a guinea pig-like rodent, about the size of a rabbit, and is very vocal – it has 21 different calls! Not so easy to see, but there nevertheless, are ibex, gazelle, wild leopard and golden jackal, mainly in the mountains around the Dead sea. There are also red fox, mongoose and the fennec fox, which is nocturnal and hunts in large groups.

Both the Israeli and Jordanian Governments have strict conservation policies to protect the remaining flora and fauna, as a number of species such as Lyre Birds, wild pig and the striped wild ass, called Onegars, have become extinct in the last hundred years or so. It will certainly pay you to take binoculars and to spend some time watching the wildlife whenever and wherever you can, for you will hardly ever fail to see something worth while.

Above left: *Oleander*

Above right: *The Black Iris of Jordan*

Below left: *Bourgainvillia*

Below right: *Anemone at Petra*